Psychotherapeutic
Intervention
in Schizophrenia

Psychotherapeutic Intervention in Schizophrenia

LEWIS B. HILL, M.D.

 THE UNIVERSITY OF CHICAGO PRESS

Chicago & London

International Standard Book Number: 0-226-33649-2
Library of Congress Catalog Card Number: 55-5128

THE UNIVERSITY OF CHICAGO PRESS, CHICAGO 60637
The University of Chicago Press, Ltd., London

This book is a report of my present conception of the possibilities and difficulties inherent in psychotherapeutic intervention in schizophrenia. This conception grows out of thirty-five years of the practice of psychotherapy, including thirty years of teaching. Both practice and teaching turned out to be techniques for my own instruction. Most of the ideas herein developed are not original. They are, rather, a precipitate of those impressions, from whatever source, which have seemed to me most useful in building up from experience a practical, coherent working theory upon which to base rational therapy. They are presented in the hope that they may serve as a map to guide the inexperienced into profitable lines of investigation, until their own observations have accumulated so that they know, of their own knowledge, the terrain in which they operate.

My indebtedness for the material upon which the book is written is primarily and principally to those schizophrenic patients who have overcome their distrust of me sufficiently to tell me something of themselves. They must remain anonymous, but I would thank them each personally.

It will be apparent to the reader that I am also heavily indebted to very many psychiatrists who have written of what they learned from schizophrenic patients and what it meant to them. I will not attempt to name the writers from whom I have learned or to select from among them those who have taught me most. They have my thanks.

In the actual writing of this book and in overcoming my resistance to doing it, I was helped, encouraged, and driven in various ways by several friends, colleagues, and companions. Among them, it is a privilege to name, and to thank particularly, Dr. Frederic G. Worden, Dr. Ilza Veith, Dr. David Shakow, Dr. Harry M. Murdock, Dr. William W. Elgin, Dr. John D. Patton, Miss Dorothy Van Dyke, Miss Louise King, and my wife. To Drs. Worden and Patton I am indebted for permission to use certain pertinent concepts of theirs.

Wherever this book is found to be in error, incomplete, or unclear, the fault is mine alone.

Lewis B. Hill, M.D.

Towson, Maryland

Contents

CHAPTER I

On Becoming a Psychotherapist

This book is about the schizophrenic patient, his psychotherapist, and particularly the therapeutic situation which
they create and in which they participate together. The
major area of concern in discussing psychotherapeutic intervention is what both the patient and the psychotherapist
contribute to this situation and the special meaning which
each finds in the contribution of the other. Most of the following discussion concerns the schizophrenic patient and
attempts to offer the psychotherapist a frame of reference
in which this patient can be understood. This frame of reference is genetic and dynamic. Such an approach has been
demonstrated, through psychoanalytic research, to be
most meaningful for the understanding of human behavior
in general. Schizophrenia is no exception to this general
rule.

What follows is the writer's point of view, his conception
of schizophrenia, which results from years of experience.
These present beliefs and understandings could not have
existed when the writer first began to see schizophrenic patients. Neither his experience of life nor his medical training prepared him to sense what these patients presented to
him, nor did he dare to think what the data that he did
note meant to the patients themselves. And he was not
alone in this inadequacy. Subsequent years of teaching

1

and supervision have shown that young psychiatrists generally require at least two or three years of living with schizophrenic patients before they can integrate their observations and experiences.

Therefore, before discussing the patient, it should be useful to take stock of the therapist himself. This is assuming that the therapist is aware, or willing and able to become aware, of his own personal experiences, of the relevant data concerning his infancy, childhood, and adolescence, and of the effect of the sum of these experiences on himself as he is at present. With or without help of psychoanalysis, the therapist will need to know himself in terms of his beginnings, his growth, and the present state of his development.

Whatever the life-experience of the physician who chooses a residency in psychiatry and then decides to qualify himself to treat schizophrenic patients, the decisions behind the choice of career may be assumed to be highly overdetermined in their motivation. Such a series of choices is derived from meanings and values arrived at by way of many experiences occurring at various ages and at various levels of conscious and preconscious activity. In general—and it should not be surprising—the resident in psychiatry finds it difficult to give clear reasons why he wants to work with psychotic patients. However, he customarily asserts that he is interested in human beings, possesses a lively curiosity about them and the way they behave, and in some way is motivated to try to help them. Of these reasons more presently.

2

On Becoming a Psychotherapist

It is obvious that many individuals who choose this field of psychotherapy are brought to their choice, among other reasons, by a profound concern about their own mental integrity or by an appalling experience of mental illness in someone very close to them. Such personal motivations, however, do not deserve the reactions they create in some observers, who are led to believe that such psychotherapists are themselves mentally ill and therefore incompetent for other work. Such a morbid view says more about the people who entertain it than it does about psychiatrists. Intense feeling of mental insecurity or of close personal tragedy involving mental illness can provide the impetus for the great personal dedication required to master the art of psychotherapy. But such intense motivation is of itself usually not an adequate foundation for the therapist's career. The therapist must also be willing and able to submit his own personal difficulties to at least as thoroughgoing study and treatment as he proposes to apply to the problems of his patient.

I remember a new resident in a certain hospital who was emphatically dedicated to helping his patients. Earnestly, he advised his first young paranoid male schizophrenics that his own simple formula would help them to behave so they could leave the hospital, get a job, buy a home, marry, and raise a family. This, he assured his patients, characterized the behavior of healthy people. That the young resident himself had not followed his own formula, had not married, did not seem to him particularly relevant to his faith in the therapeutic usefulness of his theory. His own unawareness of himself, while spectacular, may be too common for comfort in the initial stages of the psychotherapist's career. Fortunately, after two years of psychoanalysis and patient experience, the same young psychiatrist would only comment about treating schizophrenics that "you could certainly learn a great deal from the patients."

Concerning the validity of the general intentions of those who enter into psychotherapeutic careers, it can be reported that all the competent therapists this writer has known have been characterized by an interest in people, a liking for them, and a desire to help them. But it is also true that not all therapists possessing these attitudes can work effectively with schizophrenic patients. Each of these attitudes may be genuine and mature, but unfortunately each can also be a manifestation of underlying intentions that can be most disastrous to patients in therapy. The phrase "to help human beings" can both conceal and indicate motives to set one's self up as superior to and condescending toward patients, motives to dominate and control and force patients into preconceived patterns of behavior, and even motives to achieve distinction by way of morbid self-sacrifice and self-punishment. Thus the urge to help requires careful evaluation in the light of much knowledge of a therapist's over-all character, to distinguish a useful genuine sublimation from a neurotic reaction formation. It may well be that the urge to help is not so productive as is the willingness to be of use to the patient. The latter attitude is active but not domineering.

4

Being interested in people also requires a second look. Such a professed interest may be, and often is, a valid motive based in warm human sympathy. Or it may be legitimate scientific thirst for knowledge. Less fortunately, it may be a kind of infantile curiosity. If this latter is not understood for what it is and freed to develop, it can repeatedly distort the therapeutic relationship with the patient and increase the patient's already difficult problems with the therapist.

Such a variety of persons undertake to be psychotherapists that they defy adequate generalizations. This introductory chapter is attempting to suggest that the aspiring newcomer into the work must be prepared to heed the admonition, "Physician, examine thyself." The psychotherapist must be willing to find out a great deal about himself, his motives, and his attitudes. Not all his discoveries will be pleasant experiences. Risking a generalization, it may be said that he will find himself to be both more and less objective and rational in his choice of work than he has previously thought. Everyone who elects a career in psychotherapy must learn more about himself in order to be able to understand more of what his patients reveal to him. This is a bare introduction to the inquiry into the antecedents of the student of psychotherapy, indicating direction. It leaves the exhaustive search for details to each student for himself.

Once the choice of psychiatry as a profession has been made, the medical graduate who has served his general internship usually takes up a residency in a mental hospital.

The transition from medical internship to psychiatric residency is often a drastic experience intellectually and emotionally. It offers its own difficulties, disappointments, and surprises, which may be in themselves significant steps in the development of the psychotherapeutic state of mind. At the very start, the resident finds that psychiatry, although considered a medical specialty, is very different in its orientation from either medicine or surgery. For one thing, while some patients in the mental hospital may suffer from and require medical treatment for organic disease, the patients who offer most promise psychotherapeutically are startlingly different from medical and surgical patients in that they are not physically ill. In the mental hospital the resident learns that what one diagnoses is the patient himself; what he seeks to determine is how the patient as a person differs from other persons.

True, there is some diagnostic labeling of patients in psychiatry, but schizophrenia is not diagnosed on the basis of physical and laboratory examinations. Furthermore, at first the resident may assume that he can easily label his patients by imitating his older colleagues. The trouble is that, in his early months of training, when he has made his diagnostic labels, he is frequently not correct. And, to make matters worse, even if he is right, he faces the fact that he knows of no treatment for the condition he has been able to name. For a conscientious and self-respecting physician this position is not only distressing; it is untenable, and the physician must work his way out of it.

6

What defensive attitudes can the tyro assume? He may abandon psychiatry, either concluding that it is made up of nothing but words or, more modestly, that, whatever it is, it is not for him. The resident may start searching for physical symptoms of mental disease, and schizophrenia possesses many. Once long ago this writer spent a desperate summer culturing the stools of psychotic patients, hoping to find the bacterium which produced the symptoms of intoxication he had observed. More recently, many psychiatrists have turned to forms of physical therapy. Sometimes some of these are followed by clinical improvement in the patients, but still there is no proof that any form of physical therapy is specific or lastingly curative in schizophrenia. Nor do these more recent forms of therapy relieve us of the need to master psychotherapy.

If he is fortunate, the resident comes, slowly or suddenly, to the realization that his patients are not suffering from a disease as he has learned to conceive of medical diseases. At least, it has not been demonstrated that they are. Instead, one day he realizes that their affliction is disorder or dysfunction of the mind. In a book about psychotherapy this statement might seem unnecessary. Unfortunately, it is not. The mind as an object of investigation and observation, the mind as the seat of potential or actual illness and disorder, comes as a new and unwelcome concept to the inexperienced psychiatrist. There is great reluctance to believe that the mind, in and of itself, may become disordered. Almost universally, men cling to the idea that

7

their peculiarities are "due to" some outside factor.[1] Before proceeding further, it should be noted that in this writing the word "mind" is used to refer to that part of the psyche known as the "ego." If psychoses are diseases, they are diseases of the ego.

Once the resident perceives that his patients are suffering from a disorder of the ego, he receives a new impulse toward therapy. But there are still further frustrations and difficulties in store, because this concept raises more problems than it solves. True, the resident may be acquainted with dynamic psychiatry, the topography of the psyche, and the economics of the ego. But, for all his learning, it is frequently the misfortune of the resident to be guided in his efforts at treatment by prejudices acquired in childhood, by beliefs accepted before medical study began.

For example, young residents, otherwise intelligent and adequate, often work with patients on the assumption that the ego is altogether conscious. The resident assumes that two egos talking together are conscious of the same content in their conversation. All egos are considered to be more or less alike in their goals, motives, and plans. True, it is known that people vary. There are differences in intelligence, education, experience. Some people are good, others bad, some are strong, some are weak. Like people in general, patients will differ in their friendliness or unfriendli-

---

1. The writer does not intend to get caught up in the mind-body dualism. Rather, he wishes to observe that residents are frequently so caught up and that they strongly lean to the belief that mental phenomena are "caused by" physical disease. The writer prefers to think of a mind-body unity in which, when discussing psychological processes, it is best to limit one's self to psychological concepts.

ness, in their agreeability, in their stubbornness. But it takes careful investigation and painstaking self-examination for the resident to come to the conclusion that the ego of the patient is not conscious of the same important things as the ego of the physician—and vice versa.

Before this viewpoint is accepted, the resident is almost invariably impelled to offer his patient advice, suggestion, exhortation, orders, criticism, argument, and a long list of things which ought to cause a right-thinking person to be reasonable and realistic and to behave as the physician thinks he should. Which particular ones of these steps the resident elects to take can usually be seen to be related to the means used on him in his youth to acculturate him. Usually it is disappointing to the resident that the patient does not accept his help. But occasionally he does respond most gratifyingly. He does amazingly well until an issue specifically critical for him emerges. The resident is unfortunate in either case because he fails to understand what is happening. He is prone to believe that his advice, imploring, threatening, or argument has prevailed, and, when it ceases to do so, he is at a loss. It is more likely that his interest in the patient, his willingness to spend time with and to talk to the patient, have brought about some responsiveness. For a schizophrenic patient it is something that a physician tries to help and is interested in him. That the physician does not know what he is talking about at times does not surprise the patient; he is used to being misunderstood. So long as the physician's attitude is not threatening to the patient's peculiar and special defenses, he tries to express his appreciation by compliance with what he assumes the physician demands.

In actuality, the first months of residency offer many patterns of experience, even if only a few have been discussed here. But, as time passes, the resident who has a talent for psychotherapy comes to the conclusion that he does not understand the schizophrenic. Individual verbal and symbolic acts of the patient may or may not be understood. But what is most distressing is that the resident does not understand the patient as a person. Then, as he listens more carefully, the pattern begins to make sense. The resident begins to hear and see and to sense not only symptoms in the patients that contribute to the diagnosis but the fascinating revelation of the patient's life-story. He begins to see what has happened to the patient, how the latter has understood it, and what kind of a way of life he has evolved from these experiences. This growing understanding often makes the physician uneasy. For then he undergoes a startling experience and finds himself intimately in sympathy with the psychotic patient. Inevitably, the revelation of the intimate story of the patient's life arouses in the physician associations which compare his life-experience with that of his patient. The physician recognizes that the nonpsychotic ego has also experienced vicissitudes from which it, too, has emerged with prejudices, blind spots, fears, and compulsions. In the resident all these prejudices interfere with the true hearing of what the schizophrenic has to tell. And all these lacks must be recognized by the therapist in himself, leading to the inevitable conclusion that the physician himself is fearful and defensive.

There does come a time, however, when the resident is ready to compare the psychotherapeutic orientation with the older branches of medicine and surgery and to find it equally satisfying and respectable. This happens when he has had enough experience of schizophrenic patients to begin to think of them and of himself as persons who are similarly endowed with a history of experience in life, who will now react, each individual to a given situation as he sees it in the light of his experience, in the way that seems necessary or best to him. At this point the resident uses the same words—"therapy," "treatment," "cure"—that he used at the start, but he finds a new meaning in them.

This may be the point at which we might profitably turn to a dictionary and find how these important words have been defined—particularly, what are their other than strictly medical meanings. To the minds of many, including most beginners, "therapy" and "psychotherapy" are words having connotations which come to include the notion that therapists and psychotherapists are in some way exalted persons having considerably more prestige than others. Therefore, it is healthy for us to learn that the original Therapeutae were a group of either Jews or Christian monks who appeared in Alexandria long ago. They functioned either as servants or as attendants to the wealthy and were supposed to be skilled in the healing arts. With this sobering idea of our modest professional ancestry, we may profitably re-evaluate nurses and attendants in the hospital. We observe that the gifted and experienced among them can do much for patients and that they can teach us very much, if we are willing to learn, about the patients. It is a good thing to begin to practice teamwork with the nursing personnel. For the mental patient in particular, the hospital is like a family. It is reassuring to him if the hospital family functions co-operatively and consistently.

"Cure" is a word which has a definite meaning in medicine. It is appropriate when a drug or an operation is specifically efficient in eliminating a disease. In the treatment of functional mental illness there are no such specific remedies. We are accused, therefore, of being unable to cure our patients. However, "cure" also has a nonmedical history. "Cure" means "care." Not so long ago it was used in the phrase "the cure of souls." From "cure" comes the word "curate." For our purposes the word "cure" has the important implication that we are required to take care of our schizophrenics as "souls," that is, as persons. This is a broad concept. It means that we cannot treat schizophrenic patients entirely by means of scheduled appointments for the purpose of therapeutic talk. We must also know about and participate in the total hospital activity which is the patient's matrix for living. In such participation we are useful to patients, and also we are continually exposed to firsthand knowledge of how they actually do live.

"Treat" has several meanings, and only one of these is medical. Some of the other meanings are relevant to psychotherapy. One of these is "to treat cruelly, or lightly, or seriously, like a dog, or as a joke," and so on. You treat a patient according to your regard for him, and this depends upon how you understand him. Another meaning of "treat" is vital for the constructive approach to schizophrenic patients. This is "to entertain, to supply with food and drink, *as a mark of respect.*" The schizophrenic's lack of self-respect and self-esteem is a serious matter. Consequently, the interest the physician shows to him by the attention he pays to the patient's food and drink, his diversion and entertainment, and his opportunities for useful occupation can do much to improve the patient's self-regard. It may also suggest to him that the physician would be interested in his more unique personal characteristics and needs. To "treat" may also mean to subject to a process for changing the characteristics of something, as to treat hard water so that it becomes soft water. In this sense the whole hospital experience of the schizophrenic may become a treatment which preserves his soft human impulses and his ability to live in society rather than remain hard and aloof.

"Treat" also means "to negotiate with, to make treaties or arrangements with, to arrive at understandings." All these meanings, too, refer to the necessary activity of the psychiatrist in mediating between the isolated and withdrawn schizophrenic and the hostile and threatening presences he fears in his human environment.

"Treat" also has a broader meaning for artists when they describe the techniques they use to grasp and understand a subject and then translate their impressions into a satisfactory portrayal of it. It may be useful to consider how an architect who is commissioned to draw up plans for a house goes about his business. He "treats" his commission somewhat in the following manner. First, he meets the client, observes him and his family, listens to his desires, his needs, his taste, his culture, and so on. He views the lot on which he is expected to build the house and inspects the neighborhood. He probes intently to find out what sort of a house these people want, how they expect to live in it, what sort of friends they expect to entertain. He consults the deed to the property and the legal restrictions on it. He finds out how much money the client can, is willing, and ought to spend. Then, from all this information and from his experience and skill, he draws an idea which he translates into his specific plans for a house. But these plans are more than mere house plans; they are also the architect's "treatment" of a dynamic human situation.

A close parallel exists when a psychotherapist confronts a schizophrenic patient. If the reader takes this to mean that psychotherapy is a form of artistic creation, then he finds himself in close agreement with the writer. The psychiatrist is in a definite sense an artist who works with a living medium toward creative ends. He must become able to appreciate the meanings and values of the schizophrenic patient and the human environment in which he lives. And he must be sufficiently comfortable with his own responses to the patient to be able to present to him a useful description of his way of life, so that the patient may constructively increase his maturity and his acceptance of reality. But, because the therapist is perforce an artist, he is not in any

14

way excused from also being a scientist. Paralleling the development of his artistic skills, the therapist must also learn what is relevant in biology, physiology, pathology, psychology, and psychopathology, as well as in sociology, anthropology, and the humanities generally.

Within the framework of the residency itself, there is a great deal of routine doing and learning of psychiatric practice. There are important lessons to be learned in history-taking, in examining and reporting on the mental status of the patient, in the everyday care of the patient in the hospital. The content of such training has already been described adequately in many other places. It is the object of this book, on the other hand, to suggest that, while learning the formal framework of psychiatry, while doing the things that a psychiatrist does, the resident is undergoing changes in himself. He is, in short, becoming a psychotherapist. His understanding is shifting its ground, and his awareness of himself as a person is broadening. He is thus brought to the necessity of reassessing his own beliefs, attitudes, and drives. At the same time, he is becoming increasingly able to appreciate both the schizophrenic and the non-schizophrenic qualities and characteristics of the patients he is treating.

There will be more discussion of psychotherapy; but, in order that it be meaningful, it is first necessary to turn from a consideration of the therapist to the person he proposes to treat. And in order to approach the study of the patient, it is first necessary to say something about schizophrenia.

CHAPTER II

What Is Schizophrenia?

Schizophrenia is a major concern of psychiatry. This is an assertion which can hardly be questioned in terms of the number of patients involved, total loss of human well-being, and the task of caring for these schizophrenic patients. Osler once said of syphilis and hysteria that to know them was to know medicine. In terms of psychopathology, perhaps it cannot be said of schizophrenia that to know it is to understand all psychiatry. Not to know schizophrenia, though, is to be handicapped and seriously limited in one's understanding of human psychopathology in any of its fields, including the pathology of everyday life.

In this discussion I elect to consider schizophrenia as a subjective experience and to forego objective clinical description, except as a needed background for an appreciation of the experience of being schizophrenic. I must assume that you are more or less familiar with clinical schizophrenia. My comments will not carry much conviction unless you have seen or are seeing or are moved to arrange to see some real, live schizophrenic patients over a period of time, and closely enough to know something about them as persons.

As a supplement to, but not as a substitute for, this experience with a living patient, it helps greatly to read of

In so doing, we are alerted to
night otherwise escape notice,
efore our eyes. It is, as Freud
ning if you know what you are
ere is a vast literature concern-
The starting place, in my opin-
opping place, for that matter, in
as a clinical picture is the text-
ementia Praecox, or the Group
ared in German in 1911 but was
n until 1950. In Bleuler's day it
l dementia praecox as some sort
of organic disease. Bleuler, however, along with C. G.
Jung, viewed the disorder in the light of the then new
Freudian psychology. While he appears to have thought
that the ultimate cause of the disorder was probably an unknown something genetic or organic, he was the first observer clearly to say that the various symptomatic changes
were related to events in the lives of the patients, events to
which they reacted in meaningful ways.

If one speaks today not of organic diseases or only of
patients' responses to current events in their lives but of
vicissitudes of the ego, of expansions and contractions of
its boundaries, of breaches in its integrity, and of attempts
at reinstatement of ego function, one finds no difficulty in
documenting this conception from the clinical material presented by Bleuler. He saw the processes much as we see
them today. His theory could not be further advanced until

there became available recent studies of the nature and function, and of the beginnings, of the ego.

We note that Bleuler speaks of the "group of schizophrenias"; there are a variety of states which are schizophrenic. What is common to all of them is as important as are the variations. The common primary qualities of schizophrenia are two: a peculiarity of thought and a disturbance of feeling.

The difficulty in thinking is described as a loosening of associations, so that schizophrenics do not follow those rules of association which are in common use. They do produce associations so difficult for a normal person to follow that they are called "meaningless," "bizarre," and so on. Rather than predicate a theoretical brain disorder which permits random meaningless associations, I would guess that the schizophrenic processes of association are blocked according to very explicit interdictions against the occurrence of specific categories of thought. When these forbidden thoughts near realization in consciousness, they are denied and are replaced by regressively selected symbols. As suggested by Adolf Meyer years ago, if the patient's remarks make no sense to you, that is not his fault; it is yours for not learning the language. I have come to feel that schizophrenics, like everyone else, try to make sense, try to express their sense of the nature of things. For this purpose, although they have to operate within an elaborate system of denials, dissociations, and barriers against associations, they do evolve some sort of a language, often quite uniquely the invention of the one patient. This language is, in part, verbal, always attaching to certain recurrent words or phrases a peculiar connotation and often coining new words or phrases of esoteric meaning. And, in part, it is a magical sign language of gesture, posture, and other body expression, such as vasomotor phenomena.

I am reminded here of a young college woman who for some years spent her time alternately on a disturbed and a quiet ward in a state hospital. There was always some uneasiness when she was on the quiet ward because of the recurring, acute, violent explosions frequently resulting in damage to other patients. This patient spent a good bit of time on a disturbed ward when she was not disturbed just because no one knew when the next outbreak would occur. Finally, in a moment of confidence she explained an unfailing sign. When she got up in the morning, if she wore her hair in a pompadour, high on her head, that meant there would be an explosion that day. If she wore it in a knot at the back of her neck, that meant there would be no explosion. This statement of hers was tested and found to be true. An unusual way, if you like, but still a way of conveying meaning. It is interesting that for months she used this sign, although no one knew its meaning. Only once did she give verbal expression to the code by which her behavior could be anticipated.

The feeling, or affective, disorder appears superficially to be manifest in inappropriate affect, in a generally deficient affect, in unpredictable outbursts of feeling apparently not provoked by any adequate stimulus from without. Again it is my thesis, based upon experience, that, when a schizophrenic patient is known sympathetically, this judgment of his affect proves unsound. He is capable of very deep and painful affect, and it is appropriate to the situation as he experiences it. He withholds his expression of feeling intentionally, and also he avoids such stimuli as would provoke its expression. This cannot be denied; in fact, it must be accentuated that the schizophrenic does withdraw from tempting situations as a necessary defense against further injury to his ego or, as viewed by himself, against further loss of his self-esteem.

If these statements have succeeded in arousing some curiosity and a little belief that schizophrenic patients do make some sense and do, in their peculiar way, endeavor to communicate, so that you may be motivated to listen more carefully, I think that you will discover the ability to exchange meaningful observations with even quite disturbed schizophrenics. Because this matter of communication is a necessary first step without which no psychotherapy is possible, and because of the difficulties involved, I have resorted to a little joke in my teaching. I advise residents to learn "schizophrenese." It is a serious little joke, which means that one who would know his schizophrenic neighbor must devote himself to an observant participation in the mental process of his patient. This is not to abandon scientific interests. It is rather to master the art of meaningful discourse so as to have information, to have intelligence about schizophrenia before undertaking to organize one's thoughts into a theory and before pretending to wisdom. It is to make the study of psychopathology an art of appreciation of what is before you in "the experiment of nature."

At this point it is in order to state which among the group of schizophrenias I am proposing to consider. My goal has been psychotherapy in an area in which it is admittedly most difficult and, according to many psychiatrists—Freud included—impossible. I have therefore been impelled by humility and the wish to accomplish something to select the least difficult group. This does not mean that I would select those who are least clinically disturbed. It has been demonstrated repeatedly that acute catatonic disturbances of great and dramatic violence may have a better prognosis than clinically trivial and chronic schizophrenic processes.

Ease of access for therapeutic purposes is determined by the limits of ability to communicate. In acute, severe catastrophic episodes the patient may be approachable only in primary terms, such as physical care, feeding, dressing wounds, protecting from injury, and such means of expression as touch, tone of voice, body tension, and attitudes of confidence, interest, and benevolence. Still, rapport may be possible in these ways, and treatment may begin.

I exclude from these discussions autistic children, infantile schizophrenia, and those hebephrenias and simple schizophrenias which appear early and gradually, without any discoverable acute crises or reference to external events. I would also exclude those chronic, progressive paranoid states, without acute disturbances, which have, so to speak, displaced any normal psychic development in human relationship and activities. These groups are excluded because I have not had adequate experience with them. For all I know, or suspect, at least some of these patients would be understandable and approachable if I had the skill, motivation, and resources. I do not believe that any of these persons are possessed of devils or that they lack some human motivation and sense. I have found myself everlastingly busy with those patients who present only less severe challenges and who offer more chance of achievement of a goal worth while to the patient. In this sense patients who have ever been successful in something involving human relations are much more promising than those who have never succeeded at anything. It is easier to come back to something worth while than to search for it as an unknown.

I would include in this group of psychotherapeutically interesting schizophrenics all those who, however desperately ill, have had an acute onset, particularly if it occurred in the setting of acute provocation and if it was preceded by an experience of some little success as a human being. The presence of paranoid attitudes and ideas, grandiose or persecuted, does not, of itself, mean inevitable chronicity. It is only the insidious pervasion of such attitudes which promotes inaccessibility. I do include, of course, those schizophrenics whose acute episodes are mild or brief. And here we come to an issue: Does one have to be so ill as to be declared insane to deserve the appellation of "schizophrenic"? I would answer "No." "Schizophrenia" as a diagnostic label may belong only to the psychotic

22

who cannot get along extramurally. But schizophrenia the experience and the way of operating can and does occur in many persons who are supposed to be physically ill, drunk, drugged, psychoneurotic, psychosomatic, or plain normal.

Even you, for example, may recall that one of your occasional anxiety dreams was terribly vivid. It may have been about a horrible situation such as could occur in reality, or it may have been vague, unreal, weird, and fantastically strange. You awoke, got up, voided, had a drink, lit a cigarette; you took note of your body, which is certainly yours; the room, which is yours; and the clock, which indicated the early morning hour. So far we have noted nothing schizophrenic in your recalled experience. But it may also be a fact that when you awoke and oriented yourself you still felt the strange and fearful quality of the dream and sensed the presence of the dream about you. Your little routine activities did not dispel the illusion that the dream still went on. You were reluctant, or downright afraid, to return to bed and put out the light, afraid of the reality of the dream. Retrospectively, you know that you felt lonely, little, helpless, and unable to think clearly. To be honest, you, for the moment, questioned your sanity— that is, your ability to hold fast to yourself. In so far as you were for the time existing in two irreconcilable worlds of experience and in that you were alone, aghast, and awfully helpless to think or feel your way to security, you were experiencing a brief and feeble example of what goes on day after day, night after night, in the life of some schizophrenic.

There is another sort of thing which may have happened to you, the recollection of which might aid you in sensing the panic experience of the schizophrenic. It goes like this: After a day of work, which you did adequately but with some extra difficulty, tension, anger, or abstraction, you closed your office and, with a sense of relief that the day was over, you walked rapidly to the car you parked that morning. You came to the car, but it was not there. There was another car, or, more disconcertingly, no car was there. Who has not occasionally forgotten where he parked! But it is not the incident which suggests schizophrenia. It is rather the effect of the incident which is significant. You did not instantly assume that the car was somewhere else, stolen, or left in a different place by you. You just stood there, shocked, a little bit sick, a little blank, and very much upset. You did nothing, thought nothing clearly. You almost seemed not to grasp the situation. It was as if you could not recognize yourself. Slowly or suddenly you shook off the spell. You remembered or just wandered around until you found the whereabouts of the car. There are all sorts of possibilities when you find the car. You drive off gaily, a little unduly gay and cheerful; you wonder and ruminate on the occurrence; you feel shaky about driving. Can you be sure you know where you are? The lights and shadows seem strange, time and place are not very definite. Or you may just drive hastily away and forget the whole thing. What is important for a sense of the schizophrenia in it is that momentarily, while actually oriented for time, place, and person, you could not think straight,

24

you felt disagreeably strange and uneasy, you seemed to be experiencing something out of this world, and your actions were automatic rather than planned. True it is that you recovered your normal presence of mind quickly, you re-established your ego boundaries and functions, and the whole thing lost its quality of mystery and magic. Shall we say, therefore, that you did not have a minor schizophrenic experience? Is it a hemorrhage only if you bleed over a quart?

I accept this concept of the prevalence of schizophrenic instances because, except for the fact of the instantaneous, miniature, catastrophic ego failures which you and I have experienced, truly we could not appreciate at all the experience of the psychotic schizophrenic. In the same sense that the psychoanalyst tastes a little sample of his patient's anxiety or hostility or what have you, so the therapist of the schizophrenic feels a taste of his patient's devastating futility, suspicion, loneliness, fear, and hostility.

There is much more to being schizophrenic, of course. Most of it has to do with efforts at restitution. Some of these are so strange as to appear to be the illness itself. There was a man who was arrested because he was walking barefoot in the snow wearing only a nightgown and carrying a black cat at two in the morning. He was on the way to church, he said, that is, to Mass. Crazy? The police thought so. But it is not this behavior which was his essential illness. This behavior was restitutive—to confession and to Mass to regain a sense of belonging to the human family, to restore his soul. The black cat? Because the cat was black and he found it walking in the snow, and he knew how cats hate to get wet, he had carried it. This man was walking away from his home, where he lived with his mother. By going away he avoided yielding to the idea and the impulse, which was forced into his awareness, that he should cohabit with her and so beget a Christ child and save the world. This man was lonely and inhibited; he had no intimate friends, no sexual partner. His mother had suddenly become strange to him. He had gone to church for some nine days. Still the voice would not leave him alone—the voice instructing him to assault her. So he undertook, quite sensibly to him, to seek sanctuary in the church. He got arrested and in this way became a patient diagnosed as "schizophrenic."

⌐"Schizophrenia," as used in this discussion, refers to a rupture, a dissolution of the ego, a shrinking of the ego, an invasion and taking-over of much territory, which did belong to the ego, by forces which are normally excluded from it. Subjectively, this is experienced as a catastrophic event of cosmic proportions. It is terrifying. Thought, feeling, and action are taken over; the patient is dispossessed of his own mind and body. Objectively, this panic arises as a response to some rupture of human relations or of the hope which the patient may have had of them. Often this severance is a defense against the temptation implicit in the relationship.

With this statement and illustration I conclude this introduction to the subject of schizophrenia and proceed to consider the acute schizophrenic experience, which at its worst is panic and even at its best deserves intelligent recognition and appropriate treatment. I elect to begin consideration of therapeutic opportunities with the acute and dramatic panic, because it is urgent and calls for emergency care which rests upon some understanding of what is going on. If this crisis is adequately met, the therapist will be in an advantageous position to consider the very different therapeutic indications to be met in the longer-lasting, less disturbed illness of his schizophrenic patients. If the crisis is badly treated or is neglected, then the liability to chronic disabling illness is vastly increased. It is quite possible that the thousands of patients in state hospitals diagnosed as chronic undifferentiated schizophrenics are, in fact, the result of inadequately treated acute schizophrenia.

CHAPTER III

Acute Schizophrenia: The Experience and the Treatment

The acute schizophrenic cataclysm is usually described as something which has happened to the person involved, something visited upon him from outside the boundaries of his ego. It is beyond his volition or control. Patients having this experience, or speaking about it in retrospect, refer to influences, uncanny and strange events, weird sensations, and indescribable confusion. They can neither perceive nor think clearly. There are voices and visions and intense somatic sensations, often akin to sexual feeling but sensed in inappropriate organs also. It is felt that there is a system, or influencing machine, that there are poisons or electric currents, causing the fantastic disturbances. Something or someone robs the patient of his thoughts and feelings, reads his thoughts and comments upon them and him, or forces upon him thoughts, feelings, and actions which are not his own. He cannot concentrate his attention upon topics of his own choice.

Such things are bad enough, but they are not the worst of it. The patient endures unbelievable mental pain and anxiety. It appears inevitable to him that all this is part of a cataclysm or a cosmic catastrophe. In some magical way the patient is the central tragic figure in this world

crisis. Something which he must do will determine the outcome for good or bad. What this something is he does not
clearly know. He is to be a Messiah, a savior; he is to be
miraculously saved, or he is to be eternally lost.

Panic, the critical moment in the catastrophic disruption
of the usual ego functions, is, in all probability, an event of
brief duration—minutes rather than hours or days. Tremendous tension may, however, persist indefinitely if the
panic is not adequately resolved. In the panic and thereafter it seems that the patient is a passive victim, overcome
by forces from outside himself; yet he is also a participant.
Depending perhaps upon his character and his delusions,
he either submits in flaccid or rigid catatony or he goes
into violent, but poorly organized, activity. There may be
sudden changes from one state to the other. He may appear
stuporous or abnormally sensitive and reactive to noises,
lights, and real or hallucinated persons. He may submit
to, and obey, directions automatically, or he may act only
negatively, refusing all instructions, orders, or advice.

During and following panic the patient's consciousness
is restricted. Within the limited area of his awareness
things assume a vast importance. He is, himself, of heroic
proportions, and the persecutions he suffers are diabolic.
This sounds grandiose, but it must be recognized that it
is the thinking of a confused and disorganized and vastly
regressed person. It would appear that, at least in the experience of schizophrenics, narcissism—a name applied
to this grandiose state—cannot possibly mean an actual
exalted opinion of one's self or love of one's self. It must

be regarded as the compensatory denial of the sense of worthlessness and futility, of the scars of past hurts, and of the fear of impending dissolution.

Regression is a conspicuous feature of this whole process in the patient. No less characteristic of acute schizophrenia than the regression even to great depths is the unevenness of this regression. Simultaneously, the patient is oriented in the present and in the infantile past. He speaks the language of the educated adult and that of the baby. He functions partially in the here and now but also is untidy and unable to feed himself. He thinks clearly one moment and in the next expresses himself in archaic, concrete terms. Attention is flickering, memory is evanescent, and there is often amnesia for important events during the acute catastrophic disturbance. This means that there was such confusion and blurring of consciousness that the patient does not know whether such important things as sexual or murderous assaults were actually consummated or not.

Something more needs emphasis concerning the patient's endeavor to explain his disastrous condition by means of ideas of influence, poison, and, in these times, radar and electronics. It is that the whole position of the patient is that of one who is persecuted. He is distrustful of everyone and everything. He startles easily or goes out of contact when fearful things occur. This suspicion is not a new attitude, nor will it dissolve after the panic. It has been present since the beginning and will remain. Even in moments of warm appreciation and grateful co-operation, the patient may suddenly block everything because of his fear and distrust, even his strong belief that the therapist is an enemy. It may be, unfortunately, that at this moment he eliminates him forever from the company of those who can be useful to him. This may be the beginning of the end of reality for him. Some patients probably are beyond effective co-operation when first seen, but there is a painful suspicion that such a sudden rejection is usually based upon the patient's recognition of something in the doctor's or the nurse's attitude which is in psychological reality destructive to him.

Also to be recognized most clearly in the acute confusional illness, but present throughout the patient's history, is the conspicuous hesitancy and readiness to withdraw. Indeed, I have often felt that one instant the patient was with me and the next he had withdrawn. The act of withdrawing was too quick for the eye to see, and the reason for it not discoverable by me. This withdrawal takes many forms. The patient who was listening to you suddenly does not recognize your presence. He who was telling you something important stops speaking in the middle of a word. Withdrawal may be, so to speak, active or passive. The patient may walk away, resist, refuse, spit out food, or in any way be actively negativistic. Or he may just disappear into himself, hearing but not comprehending. His face may be blank, or he may whisper to himself.

We, as physicians, must recognize and anticipate certain physical events during the acute schizophrenic episode. Eating and drinking are neglected or refused, with consequent dehydration and starvation. Defecation and urination may be negativistically prevented. Physical illnesses or injuries may not be reported or admitted. Sleep may be, and usually is, suspended for days. Overactive patients exhaust themselves. Stuporous patients can go into irreversible physical collapse. Such patients do not protect themselves from cold or from burns.

Obviously such patients need not routine but special care. They are seriously ill mentally and physically. The mental state of the patient often precludes his co-operation, and his activities undo the best nursing efforts to protect him. It is not our intent to discuss the medical treatment or the feeding and hydration problems as such. Rather, we wish to limit ourselves to the psychotherapy of the situation. This means the treatment of the person who is sick rather than the treatment of the sickness.

The ability of the physician to treat an acutely ill schizophrenic will be bounded by his thinking and his feeling about the patient. His personal contribution, in terms of the life-experience and the character traits upon which he may draw, is a matter which is beyond the limits of our discussion. His thinking, however, can be considered in terms of his grasp upon the pathology of the patient, and his feelings for or against the latter may be altered by his understanding of this pathology. Therefore, before further discussion of treatment of the patient as such, we need to review several aspects of the living pathology in the patient.

Concerning the patient's ideas of cosmic meaning in his experience, it can be said that they are grandiose, persecuted, and narcissistic. These words applied to you or to me might amount to saying that we are enormously conceited; but the concept of narcissism in the schizophrenic needs to be kept close to the other concepts that we have of him. Particularly, we think that he is deeply regressed. In the light of his understanding, God and the devil may mean merely mother as the provider of the essentials of life and health and mother as the punishing destroyer. To save the world may well mean to preserve the rapport of the infant with the good mother and to renounce the bad mother. Since the regression is uneven, the ideas of special mission may derive also from an early age, when the child learned that the mother expected of him fulfilment of all her aspirations. From very recent levels of experience the sense of saving the world may mean resisting temptation to sexual and active or passive hostile acts contrary to the patient's ideals, inadmissible to consciousness except as intrusions forced upon him by enemies.

Not only regression but the great restriction of consciousness permits archaic ideas to be entertained without critical evaluation. Although the patient may use language and may handle familiar things as if he were fully conscious, the evidence is that, as Jung once put it, he is in a waking dream. Put sharply, the patient is conscious of that which is deeply unconscious in the doctor, but he is unconscious of the everyday mental content of his doctor. Rational and logical processes are faulty and unreliable. The patient's proneness to suspicion and distrust and his dim awareness of the ordinary meaning of events about him add up to no reasonable response to the physician as a friend or as professionally competent. This is, however, no reason for the physician to fail to act responsibly or to fail to explain to the patient what his relationship to him is.

The upheaval of previously repressed happenings, which are now sensed as currently real and terrible, coincides with the sinking quite out of focus of the previously conscious understanding of events, with the result that persons are misidentified and words and acts are misinterpreted. For example, a nurse said, "Let me take your temperature," whereupon the patient fought. This patient heard the words and, in her concrete, archaic way, fought to prevent something being taken away from her. Another patient—a postpartum psychotic—who had been given a transfusion in the obstetrical hospital, commented when a blood sample was taken: "They put blood into me, and you take blood out of me. You are killing me." Even the misidentifications are fleeting. During an interview a patient kept shifting her orientation according to what the doctor said. If he spoke reassuringly and gave simple directions, he was the doctor-mother; but whenever he asked a revealing question, he was the executioner. This the doctor did not at first understand.

One further fact must be underlined before we get on to treatment. It is that schizophrenic patients have, as a general thing, very severe interdictions against the erotic, sexual, and pleasure-seeking impulses common to us all. This means that they avoid in actuality all situations of temptation and that the impulses find expression only in fantasy. The disruptive catastrophe sets loose the Pandora's box of fantastic erotic impulses and sensations. These are habitually denied by the patient and now appear as something caused by, and coming from, the other person. They are polymorphous or amorphous-perverse in quality; that is to say, they come from the depths of the id. Therefore, while the patient must be handled and managed as a sick infant or as a violent adult, any such handling and manipulating will be experienced as a sexual provocation or assault. There was a patient who was so exhausting herself that to control her activity she was given an electric shock. Seen later in the day, she said that the electric treatments were helping her a great deal. Her use of the plural was picked up and asked about. She said today the treatment was more severe but was the same as those she had received every time a doctor came near her. They were felt in her genitals and radiated from there all over her; they were driving her mad.

With just these few considerations in mind, the physician can orient himself to the patient and define for himself his useful functions as a therapist. The conspicuous situation is that the patient's ego is incompetent either to perceive the environment or to act appropriately in relation to it, nor can it repress the excess of normally deeply unconscious, archaic content with which it is flooded. So the first duty of the doctor is to act personally and through the nurses as an auxiliary ego. As the ego, he must grasp the situation of the patient and devise appropriate means of survival and protection. As an auxiliary to the patient's remnants of ego, he must communicate to the patient what the latter needs to know and do. He must also aid, by direct advice and insistence, in resisting the demands and impulses which come from the depths of the patient. Concretely, this means preventing the patient from assaulting or being assaulted by other persons and from suicide or self-injury. As an example, an acutely schizophrenic young man who had been striking other patients and attendants and who had been advised by his doctor not to do that told the nurse that in order to relieve tension he had to hit something. He felt that he should hit the window. He asked her what would happen if he did. She said, "You will cut your hand if you do." The patient hit the window, cut his hand, had it sewed up, and some time later remarked to his doctor that his recovery of reason began with that incident, in which, to his amazement, he found that the nurse had told him the truth. It is a remarkable thing that the patient's ego, shattered and shrunken as it is, can reorganize itself around a nucleus which is supported by the physician and the nurse.

Before going further into the things which need doing by the physician, it is necessary to emphasize that what he does is really less important than the manner in which he does it. The bedside manner of the psychotherapist is difficult to discuss, perhaps because it is more intimately personal than is comfortable. In order that this statement should not be misunderstood, let it be said that the attitude which is recommended is carefully divested of anything resembling love-making, caressing, or seducing. As said above, schizophrenics are much too suspicious and fearful of temptation and much too sick and regressed for any such presumptions of intimacy. Yet they must be dealt with closely, directly, naturally, and without hesitation or em-barrassment.

If another personal reference is permitted, years ago I saw a pretty, young catatonic woman, who had been mute and without food for four days. I saw her in her home after three colleagues had seen her. Following these interviews, she was having nothing to do with psychiatrists and was still mute. Her terror was painful to witness. We talked. How it came about that she spoke is difficult to report, but it was in response to my observation that she was afraid, that the noise in the radiator was really there, that she was mentally sick, and that I had come to talk with her about herself. I understood that she had been drinking heavily, that her fiancé was quarreling with her, and that she was lonely. I asked whether she ever had a friend or a chum with whom she talked frankly. She whispered, "No." I thought that her throat was dry and that she should drink some orange juice. I moved over to her bed, sat on it, and helped her drink the juice. It took half an hour or so to dare to drink it. I thought that she would get more com-fortable but that she needed someone professionally trained to talk with her about her difficulties. She nodded, and I said that I would be there at two o'clock tomorrow. I also said that she must eat and drink something. She slept that night after eating supper. She spoke to her colored maid as necessary, but refused to speak to her mother. She ate breakfast and lunch. At two o'clock I appeared and was greeted with a question. It was, "Doctor, if I were to get well, would you want to sleep with me?" I answered that "sleeping with" was something which people who were well could think about.

Now the point of this story is that it is good schizophrenese, and it shows how close and how far away one must be to treat such a girl. She knew that doctors do not ordinarily sit on patients' beds. She heard an invitation, self-issued, to come back and talk with her intimately, so she got it across that she was sick—too sick for sexual interests. Also, as it later developed, she asked for reassurance. Her lover had left her in anger, having accused her of promiscuity. She needed reassurance that she was still desirable to a man. Also, she tested the doctor, both as to his tolerance of sexuality and as to his professional integrity. Our acquaintance extended over many years. Always in correspondence she stipulated that letters be signed "Affectionately"; they should not be signed "Love," for that belonged to marriage, and they should not be signed with a mere "Sincerely," for such words were used toward others.

In the course of time, pondering over the quality of the attitude of the physician toward the sick schizophrenic which is most useful, I have come to think that the requisite human interest, concern, curiosity, and warmth and helpfulness are all most safely and satisfactorily expressed in what can be called an "intransitive" mood. The patient needs to feel the presence of these qualities in the doctor but must be protected from any sense of their being imposed upon him or of their making any demand that he cannot meet. It goes without saying that the doctor, being human, notes in himself erotic interests, anger, amusement, weariness, and so on. But these also must be intransitive—that is, not aimed at the patient.

With these forethoughts about the patient-therapist situation, we may go about the treatment of the acutely sick schizophrenic. First, we must protect him physically from injury, starvation, exhaustion, and so on. In doing so, we must protect also his damaged self-esteem. What is done must be definitely and certainly done without wavering— the patient is unable to decide, and we must make decisions for him. However little he seems to understand, we must explain what we are doing. We must tell him that what we give him—his food or his drink—we, the doctor, want him to have because he needs it. If his co-operation is available, we solicit it and make approving comments. If it is not, and force is necessary, we use that force directly, certainly, carefully, and explain in the process what is being done, by whom and why.

It is useless to argue with delusions, but it is necessary to state facts in contradistinction to the delusions, and it is certainly imperative not to go along with delusions, giving them even our tacit assent as something we believe. The patient may think that the cold wet-sheet pack is a form of torture; we must tell him that it is not so intended. He may think that it is punishment for his past assaults; we must tell him that it is treatment to reduce his tension so that he may not have to be assaultive again.

A special note is required concerning feeding. Patients have many reasons for not eating. Among them are confusion and inattention, voices commanding them not to eat, ideas that the food is poisoned or is disgusting, wishes to starve as a way to emulate the martyrs, and so on. The doctor has one reason for insisting on food: the patient must live and be nourished. There are many ways to feed a patient. What can be done with one particular patient at a given moment must be learned by trial and probably by error. A patient may eat alone or only with others, in his room or only in the corridor; he may eat only if someone keeps his mind on the procedure or only if no one refers to it; it may be necessary to spoon-feed him.

Spoon-feeding is an art. One might begin to learn it by first being fed, perhaps in the course of some illness confining him to bed. Only so can one discover in how many ways being spoon-fed can be unpleasant. Then feeding a baby is an educational adventure—how fast or slow, how much or little to feed, can be learned experimentally. How to get along with the baby in the process is a more difficult thing to describe, yet it is sometimes possible to feed him without his tears or your profanity. Feeding the schizophrenic differs from feeding one's self or the baby and is a challenge in human relations. There is no clearer demonstration of the patient's lack of grasp on reality than is found in trying to feed him or to get him to feed himself. His attention must be kept or repeatedly recaptured. He needs to be told to put spoon and food in mouth, to remove the spoon and swallow the food. He needs to sense your confidence and approval. He gets the food and also, if lucky, a lesson in accomplishment.

This spoon-feeding may be a critical event. Success may be followed by rapid improvement in rapport and beginning reintegration of the patient. Failure and the need to resort to tube-feeding is often the beginning of a long, retrograde deterioration. I hope it is implicit in this discussion of feeding that the doctor feeds not only a sick baby but also a fellow human being, one whose self-respect also needs feeding.

In the matter of tube-feeding, when it is necessary, residents are likely to be preoccupied with the symbolism and to feel embarrassed or amused or otherwise irrelevantly preoccupied. Now it may be that to the patient also the tube is a phallus, but the important thing is that to the physician, and he must make it clear to the patient, the tube is a necessary means of getting the food into a patient who cannot or will not eat. It is no more and no less. If tube-feeding has to be resorted to, certainly efforts at spoon-feeding should not thereupon be abandoned, and the tube-feeding should be discontinued at the earliest opportunity.

It has been implied, and had better be said, that what is said to the patient must be truthful. If he does go into seclusion because he is dangerous to others, he should be so informed. It may be quite surprising news to him that anyone is afraid of him. If he is secluded because he is tense and is overexcited by the nearness of others, he should know that. One should learn to keep all promises made to the patient. This requires learning not to make promises which cannot be kept.

If treatment such as we are describing is successful, there come together little bits of experience which grow by accretion until there is an appreciable area of consensus. The doctor and the growing central ego of the patient conspire to deal with the illness which invades the rest of the patient. Together they evaluate the state of things, determining how much the patient has gained and what is yet to be gained, how much progress may be made, and what are the probabilities of some regressive episodes. As Ferenczi once said, it is not so bad to be crazy if someone is with you who knows the way back. Good treatment of the acute illness is the process of being with the patient and knowing the way back.

What has been said of feeding can be applied to all the daily happenings to the patient. Bathing and dressing offer occasion for support of that bit of the patient's ego which is intact. The ward activities and the presence of other patients may need explaining. The patient usually requires some direction and incentive to constructive relationship and activity. In general, it is not helpful to try to push acutely ill patients into things. Even as they appear to have cleared up their confusion, they are still tense, uncertain, and easily disturbed and tired; but it can be noted which nurses and patients they like and what activities do interest them.

Frequently the patient, on getting enough better to look back on the horror of the episode, undertakes in one massive act to deny and cover over the whole experience. He wants to forget it and go home. It is characteristic schizophrenic concrete thinking that one is sick in a hospital— that is, sick because in a hospital. If one leaves the hospital, one leaves the sickness. It is possible at this point, however, if the physician has been in close and useful attendance, for him now to exert his authority and influence to get the patient to proceed slowly and to review what has happened. In this way recurrence may be avoided and perhaps something valuable salvaged from the experience of the illness.

While the foregoing treatment is in process, the physician needs to be observant. The treatment itself is paced by the patient's often slight indications of his reactions to it. Timing is of the greatest importance. Its success or failure depends upon the physician's correct apprehension of his patient's tension and preoccupations. Progress should not be too rapid or too slow. Observant physicians are gaining more than cues to immediate treatment as they observe the patient. They are learning things which it will be necessary to know in the later phases of treatment, at which time the patient may not be confiding them. One young woman, so excited upon admission as to require seclusion, began to menstruate in a few days. This, in itself, was a little unusual. Menstrual function is often suspended during acute psychosis. This girl insisted, whenever a doctor appeared, on waving her Kotex at him. It was obviously a message of some sort. Her immediate past history was that she had become confused, had run away, and had been picked up by a truck-driver. He made advances to her but accepted her money and put her down sexually untouched. Otherwise, there was no known history of sexual activity. But when she was asked what the Kotex meant, she explained it. A few days before the truck-driver episode she had gone to a large dinner party in a hotel. There a man had taken her to his room and seduced her; the Kotex was her sign that she was not pregnant. It is implied here that this patient might have tried to seal over this (to her) disgraceful episode as she improved, but the fact that the doctor was curious about the meaning of the Kotex signal led her to divulge it, to her considerable relief.

During the dramatic illness patients exhibit various peculiar postures, gestures, and grimaces. They refer to sundry persons, places, and events. They mistake nurses, doctors, and other patients for former acquaintances. All this needs to be noted because it is not chance, meaningless stuff; it is a form of free association, referring to the central conflict of the patient, to the event leading up to the illness, and to the history leading up to that event.

This observation brings us to consider why a particular patient became acutely ill upon a certain day. It focuses our attention upon the period of time immediately preceding the break with reality. The assumption is useful that the break occurred because the reality was intolerable. Of these things we will think later; but at present, while considering the acute illness, we do want to remember that it occurred as one dramatic link in a chain of events. These critical events are in the patient's mind. It is obvious that the distressing symptoms need emergency care for which rapport is essential; hence it is not advisable to try to extract from the patient confessions that he is not prepared to make. When a house is on fire, it is foolish to engage the owner in a discussion of his habit of dropping lighted cigarettes.

But from the available history clues may be had. Occasionally a patient tells outright what has happened. It may be that his story is so direct that nobody believes him. More often, his illusions are so tenuous as to be missed by all but the most observant. The relatives and friends rarely know what it was that happened about which the patient lost his reason. A general formula may be of some help to us. It is that in some way the patient experienced something altogether forbidden to him by his own self-regard. This something then persisted in his mind as a craving or an idea completely foreign to him yet compelling. In his retreat from it he fell into confusion, flight, and panic.

Both for our better understanding of the acute illness, so that we can reconstruct it with the patient, and for our further therapeutic endeavors, aiming not alone at prevention of recurrence but at the freeing of the patient for a fuller and less lonely life, we need to investigate the situation in which the illness occurred. We do find that the situation was dire and dreadful, and we also find that the patient got into it only as an end result of his previous way of life, going back at least to his infancy.

We will now turn our attention to that way of life which frequently eventuates in an acute schizophrenic illness.

CHAPTER IV

On Being a Person Prone to
Schizophrenic Episodes

The acute schizophrenic break with reality is the outcome of a situation involving the patient and someone else, in which situation the patient felt that a vital human relationship was disrupted. It often appeared that the break was related to some experience of temptation and can be regarded as a flight from that. We may now attempt to add some further description of the situation at the time preceding the break. First, it can be observed practically always that the patient was severely disappointed in the other person and became very suspicious of him. Even more regularly the patient was disappointed in himself, so that his already dubious self-respect was very badly damaged.

The beginning of the buildup of a critical situation is not at all necessarily in events that one would expect to be disturbing to a normal person. Quite to the contrary, it may appear that the patient was taking or was about to take a step forward in his maturing and developing, in his emancipation from youth and from family influences. Some of the events reported as commonly preceding the catastrophic break are the patient's first separation from home to go to college or to military service or to a job, or into marriage. Other such events are the near-completion of a year of college or near-graduation or impending promotion in work or, again, marriage or parenthood.

What all these situations have in common includes the fact that they are steps toward independence and change of status in the direction of maturity. It is in this sort of promising phase of progress that something begins to go wrong with the patient. He begins to withdraw and be pre-occupied. His ability to study, to work, to consort with others, diminishes. He is uncertain, suspicious, and filled with obsessive doubts. Thinking becomes difficult, sleep is disturbed, or occasionally he begins to sleep late into the day, neglecting his duties. There are often hypochondriacal concerns which may indicate an alteration in the patient's satisfaction with his own anatomy. There is some degree of depersonalization or feeling of unreality and doubt of one's sanity. All these changes in the patient add to his feeling of futility, his lack of self-confidence or of trust in others.

In so far as the pathology is purely schizophrenic, there is no feeling of depression—that is, of sadness. Nor is there psychomotor retardation. Rather, there is a futile inertia which can be punctuated by periods of intense activity. In the absence of sadness, the feeling of the patient is more correctly described as that of amazement and puzzlement. In history-taking we often hear from the patient or a relative that there was a depression, but this is a layman's misconception of the term which must be investigated to see whether they mean depression or withdrawal and apparent indifference, futility. It must be remembered that schizophrenia may exist underneath a depression, so that the clinical picture is schizo-affective.

It is possible, and happens often, that all this has been going on in the patient for days, weeks, or months before anyone notices it. Such patients are not very close to anyone; they often conceal their difficulties. Occasionally they ask for help, but they usually do so in such a halfhearted manner as to lead to refusal. One patient actually sought a psychiatrist, made an appointment, and, on arriving, presented himself as so disinterested and incapable of meeting any of the requirements of treatment as to cause the psychiatrist to assume that the patient was drugged, deteriorated, or actually completely indifferent to the procedure. The psychiatrist, therefore, did not undertake treatment of the patient, who promptly went into an acute disorder. It is the duty of a psychiatrist to assume that anyone who consults him has some need and that his denial of it is part of his illness. In the instance just cited surely the psychiatrist did not "cause" the acute psychosis, but equally surely he did participate in the situation to the patient's disservice. It is a good thing to keep schizophrenia in mind when the clinical picture is unclear.

One or many little episodic disturbances may be weathered before there is an overt psychotic illness. Sometimes they go on until the patient fails in school, is fired from his job, is deserted by his spouse or fiancée, and is finally recognized to be quite sick. But frequently the tension gets unbearable, and the patient suddenly tries to do something about it. He tries flight. This may be a suicidal attempt, in which case the suicide is a matter not of depression but of dramatic futility or of the obeying of hallucinated orders. The flight may be a going-home, or it may be a more or less dramatic flight to a strange place, a big city, or just wildly across the country. This flight can end, and often does, in panic, confusion, and hospitalization. Sometimes the flight is into seclusion in his room and absorption in somnolence.

Some patients report that during this wretched experience they were seduced or at least were approached by someone with seduction or perversion in mind. It is certainly true that some of these reports are of actual happenings. The patients do manage, in their effort to break the tension, to find and expose themselves to someone who does introduce them to some form of sexual activity. The experience usually leads to rapid dissociation. It is regarded as distasteful to the patient and yet persists as a fantasy and a craving which seems not to be his own. Most of the accounts, however, of seduction amount to a very uncritical acceptance by the patient of evidence to support his fantastic fears. What seems certain is that the patient felt some urge within himself with which he was not familiar or comfortable. He often blames it upon the supposed sexual meaning of the behavior of someone or other.

We may speculate on the meaning of an experience such as this which leads into acute catatonia. There are two ways of regarding it, which are not actually exclusive of each other. The question is how much of the behavior is to be understood in one way and how much in the other. One way of describing the patient's behavior is to say that, faced with more real responsibility and requirement than he could accept, the patient ran away in the only direction in which he could run—that is, backward into earlier, less differentiated, more dependent and inadequate behavior. The other way to state the same thing, with a different implication, is to say that the patient, lacking the ego function necessary to carry on, was exhausted by his efforts and then was unable to keep up the barrier against the unconscious, which invaded and took him over by assault, so that what was fantasy suddenly became reality, and what had been reality was temporarily abandoned.

The former of these views gives the patient's ego credit for the ability to defend itself by denial and retreat, to endeavor to save itself by sacrificing much of its integrity. The latter view is that the ego of such a patient is lacking in drive, in force, and in cohesiveness and is actually a victim of the assault from the unconscious. I think that patients exist to justify either one of these views but that most patients can be seen as involved to some extent in both the voluntary and involuntary regressions. Objectively, it is noted that sometimes the environmental events in which the patient became involved were unusual. Sometimes the patient had recently been physically ill, but often the opening moves toward acute illness occurred in situations which would not be stressful to normal persons. I wish to emphasize again that sometimes the break seems to come just at the point at which the patient is about to be, in reality, quite successful. It would appear that there is some factor operating within him to destroy his independence.

We may ask, therefore, what sort of a person it is who has to get caught up in the avalanche of regression. I am inclined to believe that he is one who has found the problems of living in reality all too painful. He has had much experience and has acquired considerable skill in the technique of quietly slipping away into fantasy which, in its depths, is regressed to the vagueness of infancy. An evidence of this practice is the somewhat withdrawn and preoccupied habit of these patients.

Whether the avoidance and the evasion are the result of ego deficiency or of especially heavy ego burdens, it would seem that there is a long history of systematic denial of certain—for the patient—specific issues and situations. What has happened is that, rather than develop a growing ability to test and to live in reality, the patient has become adroit at ignoring embarrassing parts of it and has become dependent upon this ability to maneuver himself in a schizoid way. This has worked well enough to prevent acute schizophrenic collapse in the face of repeated minor difficulties of youth and adolescence. But it fails to be a useful device when the life-situation becomes more decisively serious, when the patient's actual incompetence as a person can no longer be concealed from himself.

I think there is an analogy in all this to the rather generally better-understood performance of the alcoholic. He has for some years escaped the too unpleasant by way of chemical depression of ego functions, particularly self-criticism. In spite of, and because of, his long exploitation of this technique he eventually brings about a critical situation, tries to evade it by way of alcohol, and is caught up in disastrous failure. He no longer drinks to face life; he lives to drink to be oblivious. The chemical effect of alcohol may be loosely equated to the ego deficiencies of the schizophrenic. Withdrawal and regressive mental activity, like alcohol, can be exploited to reduce the acuteness of conflict and the feeling of anxiety until they become a way of life. Such a way of living sets up increasingly grave real crises to be met, until finally one of them carries such anxiety and tension that there is a massive conflict—a massive, completely involuntary collapse of large parts of the ego into relatively undifferentiated infantile states.

What is lost is an adequate grasp upon the perceivable environment, particularly the human environment, and the ability to evaluate its meanings. Particularly, one's critical function disappears, and the most archaic and primitive of explanations are accepted. What takes over is the bureaucracy, on the one hand, of conscience in its infantile terms, and, when that fails to control, the Pandora's box of infantile forbidden wishes and needs. What was a conflict in a real situation has now become a raging war between these two opposing activities—those promoting the achievement of infantile wishes and those interdicting any and all reference to them. The ego is so busy observing this conflict and striving merely to survive in the middle of it that the testing of reality becomes a secondary, un-

important, and, one might say, negligible concern. Antici-
pating later reference to the superego, it may be said here
that, when the superego validates an ego impression or
idea, there is no further sense of doubt, no need to test; the
impression or idea is accepted as true. Current events have
almost no current real meaning and are understood only in
their archaic implication.

From this point of view there are some interesting things
to be noted about the young person who is on the way to
clinical schizophrenia. Some of these appear to be the
peculiarities of one who, by both endowment and infantile mismanagement, has tried to be like a normal person
but has tried even harder to be faithful to certain infantile
ideals, desires, and understandings. These have to do,
essentially, with his survival, which is dependent upon the
survival of one who cares for him, so that they have to do
with the maintenance of the infantile mother-child symbiosis. The result is that his life has been severely restricted, limited, and invaded by the requirements of his
parents' conscious and unconscious conflicts and drives.
Anything in the unconscious of the parent which would
produce anxiety must become a preoccupation of the patient in order to keep down parental anxiety and thereby
reduce his own distress. I have mentioned elsewhere the
thought that the recurrent ideas of Messianic mission, of
world salvation, and, in its milder forms, of reorganization of the world, economically, politically, and so on,
have something to do with the basic necessity of the schizophrenic to consider what ways will further his chance to

survive. Since his infancy his major concern has been to save an environment, a matrix, in which to live. If he does not succeed in that, he dies or is eternally punished.

The life-stories of those who later become schizophrenic support the belief that, in general, they were always good, clean, obedient, respectful, adoring and so on. Careful investigation reveals, also, that they had a good many difficulties—night terrors, thumb-sucking, nail-biting, enuresis, sleepwalking, or difficulties with food. These, however, have usually been mastered by a determined mother. One would think that in this setting there must also be present a desperate fear of the parent, so great that it prevents expression of hostility; there must, of course, be great hostility. In this sense a good bit of the schizophrenic behavior can be seen as vengeful in a somewhat sly manner, since direct assault upon the mother is unthinkable except in acute psychosis. The whole problem of the schizophrenic can be seen, then, as that of a small child who is utterly dependent upon a person by whom he feels persecuted and who is, in his opinion, unstable and uncertain. Let us now consider what consequences there are in the life of such a person, flowing from the pre-emptive insistence upon the problem of survival by means of preserving the mother.

This calls for a review of some of the evidence having to do with the relationship of schizoid and schizophrenic patients to the pleasure principle and the reality principle as enunciated by Freud. Before doing this, I want to make one comment concerning the use of the word "pleasure" in this formulation. The word used by Freud was, of course, not "pleasure." He was speaking of a physiological experience of reduction of tension, which comes to be felt as good and desirable. He was not speaking of what is commonly implied in the American language when we speak of pleasure-seeking. Furthermore, this concept arose while studying hysterics, who are known for their readiness to yield to efforts to reduce tension, whereas the reality principle seems to have more to do with more serious persons.

The reality principle is an amendment, or modification, of the pleasure principle. Perhaps we should first consider how the schizophrenic relates himself to this matter. In brief, those who are likely to have schizophrenic episodes handle some reality quite adequately. They are frequently competent in classwork, in school; some are quite competent athletically; some show considerable artistic ability; and many of them for some years of their lives give the appearance of being socially adequate. However, the outstanding impression one has is that the abilities which they have, and exercise, do not seem to be built together by them into a practical plan, which can be carried out step by step to the goals commonly regarded in this society as desirable. As one example, a schizoid student who, at the age of thirty-seven, was still taking courses in a university where he had done some little teaching, having otherwise been unemployed, had acquired sufficient credits all together for at least two doctorates, except that he had carefully avoided, in all the years, learning enough German to meet the requirements; and, although he had the material at hand, he had never got around to writing his thesis. To make matters worse, the credits which he had accumulated were in such assorted subjects, many of them rather abstract, that they did not qualify him to teach in any of the usual departments to be found in the universities. This same man arrived at the age of thirty-seven before he undertook to carry out what he regarded as one of his active sexual desires. There was a fantasy that he would devote three years to intercourse with a different girl each night. This would add up to about a thousand girls, which he felt would make him about even with other men his age. However, at that time he had not even held hands with a woman. When he did so, he found himself quite promptly trapped and married to a woman with whom he could not get along. From then on, his career was one of romantic idealism, spasmodic efforts, no actual accomplishment or achievement of position for himself, and no enduring alliance with any woman.

The poor planning of these patients is shown in many ways. There was a woman who discovered only in her late thirties that, in view of her intelligence, her education, her physical health, her family position, and her wealth, it would be a good idea for her to procreate; clearly, she would produce a superior child. To this end she set about looking for a husband and picked a man in his early twenties, whom she consulted, since he was a psychologist, for advice in the matter of locating an intelligent, healthy, desirable father for her child. As a result of one interview, she became convinced that this young psychologist was the man for her, and it was with great difficulty and only after some months of distress that he managed to extricate himself from her insistence. She was incapable of grasping that he did not love her and did not want to marry her. This is a rather extreme example of what has occasionally been called the thinking introvert, which, in such extreme form, amounts to a sort of ambulatory schizophrenia.

One gets the impression, in dealing with these prepsychotic schizoid persons, that they are interested in ideals rather than in practical ambitions. They carry longer, and entertain more seriously, the intention to write a great novel, than do the majority of other adolescents. However, they frequently do not learn to type, nor do they acquire any experience which would equip them to write. They are often interested in social and group activities, but this interest is, again, theoretical and not something in which they actually are capable of achievement.

In another setting one feels that these patients are interested in principles or abstract ideals rather than in persons. Such preschizophrenic characters reject the need to offer a service to a dear, close friend because their ideals do not approve of the jam into which the friend has got. It is disconcerting to find that one who has seemed to be close to you can so readily lose interest. There is a result of this which is embarrassing to the schizophrenic. He fails to make close friends, fails to keep them, and, frequently, when he does wish to accomplish something, discovers that he has no connections available to serve his purpose. It follows, of course, that many of these patients are quite indifferent concerning money and its usefulness. They do not take steps to acquire or to keep it. One might wonder what these patients are thinking about in the world as it is organized about them today. An answer would be that they are thinking about independence versus dependence. They are preoccupied with emancipating themselves from something or other. The something or other includes family and home, the religion in which they were brought up, a parochial culture, and sometimes any dependence upon anybody for anything. Many plans are made, but these plans are obviously impractical and often are not even undertaken. They could not be carried through if they were, so that the patient is always falling back into a dependent and subordinate position, which is always an injury to his self-esteem.

Further acquaintance reveals that these patients have a marked preference for ideas rather than for action. They would rather think about people and think in terms of some psychological jargon than be actively engaged in interchange with people. The interest in ideas extends to a considerable investment in the meaning and values of words, which they tend, even before the acute illness, to use in a somewhat peculiar and individualistic manner. From this it is a short step to interest in theories and philosophies, and from here one may readily progress into a sort of pseudo-philosophy.

It must be said that a good many schizophrenics have

excellent minds and do acquire considerable training, so that, in addition to the rather fantastic philosophizing and theorizing, many of them do become educated and are quite competent in certain fields of science. There are a good many instances of men who have been famous for their serious ability intellectually, until, with advancing age, they exhibited the superstition and mysticism which we associate with schizophrenia.

The lack of a keen sense of reality is shown also by these patients in a certain quality of timelessness, apparent in their thinking, planning, and actual behavior. They are living according to the principle that life is not yet real; this is not *it*; it is all a sort of make-believe or "as if."

These characteristics of the ambulatory schizophrenic are those with which we are familiar as part of the obsessional character. There are doubtless other bases upon which patients become obsessional, but the obsessive devices are certainly appropriate and commonly used by schizoid people to protect themselves from the harsh realities of their own feelings about people and things as they are. Their obsessive character, with its reaction formations, permits them to avoid facing real conflict, permits them to be unaware of their hostility toward others, justifies them in avoiding fights—even when they are indicated—and also permits them to avoid competition. The obsessive character is a useful device which stands between many persons and a frank psychotic disintegration.

These difficulties which have been noted in the application of the reality principle to living would lead us to wonder what these patients do about the underlying pleasure principle. If they cannot manage the amendment, does that mean that they, in their regression, then become free to follow the pleasure principle unchecked? The answer to this is, with the probable exception of the hebephrenic, definitely "No." Schizophrenic patients as a group give the impression of being less interested, or successful, in pursuing pleasure than any other group of patients I know. Even the depressed patient gets a certain cruel pleasure out of the suffering which he can fantasy he is inflicting upon those near and dear to him. The schizophrenic is not without his vindictiveness, but his capacity to delight in it, as most of us experience pleasure in retaliation, is extraordinarily limited.

It is natural for one to think rather directly from pleasure to sexual matters, and this may be an area in which to check the state of the schizophrenic in relation to pleasure. It can be demonstrated that schizophrenic patients as a group have masturbated less, have begun later in life, have had more conflicts about it, and have more often given it up or converted it into a compulsive battle than other, more normal persons. It is not uncommon to find the schizophrenic patient who has reached the late teens before ever experiencing masturbation which he can remember. Part of this delay is because such patients are not very social, have not belonged to gangs or groups, and have not been intimate with chums, so that they have had to learn it for themselves. However, a good many nonschizophrenic youngsters have managed to learn it for themselves while still very youthful. It is to be noted also that a good many schizophrenics, if they have accepted some masturbation as necessary, have given up even that little outlet shortly before the steps which lead into an acute psychosis.

Most schizophrenic patients and preschizophrenic candidates are capable of heterosexual activity—that is, they do not suffer from the impotence and frigidity which are so common in hysterics. However, this freedom from encumbrance does not result in very much heterosexual activity. Premarital relations are more often autistic than actual. A great many schizophrenics never marry. Many of them carry on very little sexual activity in their married life. It is not uncommon to find schizophrenics who have tried heterosexual activity for one purpose or another but have not found it worth continuing. There appears to be, actually, a deficiency in the sexual drive. The sexual history furnishes a clear example, however, of the way in which the schizophrenic, in his evasion of reality, enriches his fantasy. There are quite commonly rich and elaborate, fantastic, romantic heterosexual interests. Some of these are quite abstract; others are rendered safe by being attached only to the person of a movie actress who is actually on the other side of the country or to a character in fiction. They are also frequently attached to clergymen, physicians, teachers, and so on, and are, in general, kept autistic—that is, they are unknown to the object.

It is clinically well known that schizophrenics are very

sensitive in the area which may loosely be called "homosexual." This sensitiveness, however, amounts principally to fears and preoccupation with the thought that someone else might think the patient homosexual or with efforts to determine in self-defense which persons in the environment may be homosexual. The patients make elaborate efforts to avoid the implication of being homosexual. It is so common for the fear of the patient who goes into panic to include some homosexual content that these panics have even come to be known as "homosexual." However, none of this would argue that the patient is actually driven, himself, toward homosexual activity. Rather, all his fantasies are those of being passively exploited by someone else who is sexually aggressive. I have the impression that when schizophrenic patients do enter into homosexual activities and accept them as a way of carrying on, they do not do so primarily because of their own legitimate drives. Their behavior is more probably a means of making themselves useful and important to someone, a means of achieving the appearance of intimacy, and an effort to monopolize someone. It is common experience that those schizoid persons who do undertake to operate in terms of homosexual maladjustments live a very difficult life because of their jealousy. Jealousies are of course related to hate rather than to love. Such patients also suffer anxiety and fear of loss of the partner. They must also bear their humiliation and try to develop the necessary compensatory attitudes, a task often beyond their abilities.

It is my impression in general that schizophrenic people have not any real faith in sexuality as a necessary thing, a good thing, or a workable thing in the process of surviving in this life. It has been the experience of certain gifted observers, notably Federn, that schizophrenic patients who have recovered from an acute psychosis and in that way have become somewhat like these patients under discussion who have not yet had an acute attack frequently relapse if they undertake to indulge freely in sexual matters. It would seem that they cannot support an investment both in their own ego and in sexual activity.

There are exceptions, clinically, to the rule that schizophrenics are not sexually active. These are patients who are driven in their flight from feared heterosexuality or even feared masturbation, both of which have incestuous implications apparent to the patient, into compulsive homosexuality. Others are driven by their fear of homosexuality into compulsive heterosexual activities. In these cases, certainly, there is little reference to the pleasure principle. It is a rather desperate compulsive maneuver to avoid disaster.

Another area in which the schizophrenic's interest in the pleasure principle may be tested is that of his relation to food. Although mothers at first deny it, frequently it is learned that schizophrenics had some difficulty and were feeding problems in their infancy. A considerable number of these patients throughout life have carried food idiosyncrasies, have suffered from allergies to certain foods, and have had aversions to common articles desired by others. I have known a number of patients who commented that they did not like fat women—particularly full-busted women—and then in the same conversation, but without seeing the relevance, have remarked on their dislike of custards, gravies, thick soups, oysters, and so on. It is a serious problem, with the acute schizophrenic, to get him to eat at all. He is quite likely to think the food is poisoned, and this is not entirely a new idea. In his prepsychotic days he was a little indifferent to food and a little afraid of it. He ate to live rather than living to eat and frequently had rather elaborate eating rituals, having to pick over his food obsessively. The attitude of schizophrenics toward alcohol is also peculiar. While some of them drink considerably and while a good many alcoholics show schizophrenic content in their acute disturbance, in a general way schizophrenics are not particularly interested in alcohol. It would seem that they already suffer from defective ego abilities and are afraid of alcohol because it might produce panic in them.

We might further consider the schizophrenic's interest in pleasure in terms of his physical activity. There is a well-recognized type of schizophrenic of athletic build and great athletic ability, who undoubtedly has pride in his muscular skill. A number of schizophrenics like to swim, and a number are interested in dancing, particularly interpretative and ballet dancing. Many of them have a good bit of ability in music and artistic expression, but in general the pleasures which they describe are somewhat idealized and abstract. Frequently the athletic endeavors are—from the point of view of health—either to keep themselves strong or to keep themselves exhausted so that they will not be sexually disturbed. Quite a number of these schizoid patients are definitely ascetics, living very frugal, abstemious, and restricted lives.

Reference has been made to the translation by schizoid persons of their various interests from realistic activity to fantasies. One might wonder whether, in the world of fantasy, they achieve adherence to the pleasure principle. There is some evidence that schizophrenic and schizoid people, like certain young children, get much pleasure out of skin eroticism and out of visual impressions such as are gained when viewing the sun through nearly closed eyelids. It is probable that there is a good bit of a certain kind of pleasure which is indescribable and cannot, therefore, be shared with others. There was a schizophrenic painter who made a good living at commercial art and then for her own satisfaction painted, sometimes for many hours continuously, but never showed any of her paintings to anyone, not even to her closest friends. Under no conditions had she thought of selling any of these expressions of herself. She was, in fact, unable to paint in the presence of anyone and unable to interrupt her painting for social exchanges of any sort. She either did not eat or ate only a little bite alone during the days she painted.

The fantasies which take the place of reality in these patients are very interesting. Some of them have a religious overtone, a mystical quality; others are quite concrete. I recall one patient who, being afraid that the house was wired, would not talk to me in her home but insisted on walking in the garden, through which ran a stream. To my moderate distress she picked out of the stream a little red scorpion, a tadpole, and a frog and insisted that I hold them while we talked. It developed that this girl lived what to her was her real life out in this garden. She was on intimate terms with all the cold-blooded animals and a good many of the plants. I made some comment upon the absence of human beings, and the girl informed me that she would have supposed that I, a psychoanalyst, would interpret the scorpion—a little red fellow—as having to do with her father's penis. She went on to add that she could not tolerate her father in any form and was glad to know that I had not regarded the scorpion as representing him. She then went on to explain which of the cold-blooded animals represented her mother. One turtle in particular reminded her of mother in its well-incased defensiveness. Others of the animals represented a sister and a dead brother. I never found out which of them represented me. This girl had some ability in writing poetry, none of which made any reference to human beings other than herself.

An intended conclusion from this discussion is that schizophrenic patients, long before their acute illness, function in a fashion which shows that they have not developed in the manner of psychoneurotic and normal people in terms of a primitive pleasure principle, which comes to be interpreted and modified through experience with the environmental realities. They operate clearly upon some other principle, which supersedes and transcends the motivation which applies to us. They are interested in values and meanings which are not obvious to us. They have an extensive, systematic avoidance and system of denials by which they evade entanglements with the reality which is what makes life worth living for the rest of us. They are dedicated clearly to some unrealistic goal—at least, unrealistic to us. This leads to the statement of what has been obvious in all our approach to the schizophrenic: schizophrenics, as compared with other people, are extremely serious and are interested in meaning. They are trying to find some unifying principle, trying to find some sort of peace, symmetry, or harmony in the world. Since it is not in the real world, they look for it elsewhere.

It becomes our task, if we are to treat schizophrenics with some understanding, to pursue this question of the principles upon which schizophrenics seem to run their lives. To this end it is expedient to consider what may be different in their experience of early infancy and in the stages of their ego development from the experiences of normal children in the same early months.

CHAPTER V

On Infancy—the Period of
Becoming a Person

Freud's research into the meanings of symptoms of hysteria led him, of course, to the beginnings of the symptoms and the conditions existing at their onset. His path then led into earlier hysterical episodes, all strung along on the hysterical character structure and way of living of his patients. He and, particularly, his followers have traced the beginnings of hysteria into the very early years of life and have been, of late, investigating the early infancy of babies to learn in what steps they became persons. Out of these studies has grown a theoretical formulation of the events resulting in the existence of an adult ego. This way of thinking about mental health and illness offers so much basis for comprehension of the rationale of child care, of education, and of psychotherapy that psychoanalysis is regarded by an ever increasing number of psychiatrists as a basic discipline in their training for their work.

I have grown up in this tradition. My conception of the nature of schizophrenia includes ideas of immaturity, of fixation and distortion of interests and concern at various early levels of experience, and of consequent impoverishment of the ego, resulting in failure to live in current reality and in regression to areas of blocked development and persistent infantile interests.

I think it evident that acute schizophrenic illnesses occur in the lives of those who are predisposed to them by virtue of the pre-existing schizoid character structures and defensive, restrictive, limited ways of existing. I believe that an acute schizophrenic catastrophe occurs, ordinarily, in the life of one who has experienced several similar, if milder, episodes and that these can frequently be traced back into the earliest months of life. In order to appreciate the situation of the schizophrenic and to grasp the therapeutic tasks, difficulties, and possibilities of that situation, we need some facts and ideas about these facts in the infancy and development of these patients.

I do not expect to find any one discrete etiologic factor. I do expect to find some significant differences, at least in degree if not in kind, between the infantile experiences of schizophrenics and those of other children. To recognize what is different means, first, to know what is usual. It will facilitate our discussion of the infancy of those who become schizophrenic if we now review the general notions which are held concerning the processes and stages by which one becomes a normal person. While we are on the lookout for differences, it is to be expected that, in large part, we will find that children who become schizophrenic pass into, if not through, the same stages and experiences in infancy as do other children and that they are in many ways quite like these other, healthier ones.

Hence I propose to indicate the simplest scheme of the

process of becoming a person that will serve our needs. This is admittedly and intentionally not an attempt to formulate a detailed, documented account of infancy. It is no more than the precipitate of my observations, readings, and thinking about child psychology. It becomes, thereby, merely a working outline of a clinician's notions of how, approximately, things probably are in infancy, things which have to do with how life will be lived in the later years of the infant. This outline seems to be derived largely from psychoanalytic concepts, but it is not intended, in any sense, to be a statement of psychoanalytic doctrine. There is extensive borrowing from other sources, among which the reader will recognize Gestalt psychology, Pavlovian psychology, and the works of Federn and Weiss, of Sullivan, and of Fairbairn, to mention only a few.

Whatever may be the physiologic implementation, living organisms come into being and behave as if according to plan or design or purpose. The most general purposes would seem to be existence, survival, growth and development, then differentiation and integration, and eventually perpetuation of the design for all of this. To this end, the organism functions with marvelously complex sufficiency, provided only that certain disasters are avoided. There are built-in devices for the anticipation, detection, and avoidance of harm. The newborn child sleeps, eats, grows, develops, and differentiates. But its sleep is interrupted by warnings of starvation, chilling, loss of support, or violent external commotion. Pain, discomfort, hunger, and fear interrupt sleep and set in motion efforts to restore comfort and safety. Of course, babies are not omniscient or omnipotent, and various disasters are not anticipated or effectively avoided; but most babies in this civilization, having a great deal of maternal help, do survive and grow.

The various organs and systems of organs which comprise the organism are interrelated and integrated by means of nervous and hormonal systems which function as if they were, within limits, wise and purposeful—indeed, as if built into their structure and function were the survival values of phylogenetic experience. The nervous system appears to operate in two parts: one sensory, one motor. But for our purposes—those of explaining to ourselves the meaning of the behavior of a person—it is good to consider, as do the Gestalt psychologists, that the nervous system is in fact sensorimotor, functioning as a unity which appears to be motivated by needs and drives originating within the organism, to the end that these needs may be satisfied through interaction with the environment. It is not our intent to explore neurophysiology as such; we wish only to start somewhere with some foundation upon which to build our conception of psychic function. From Gestalt psychology we wish to borrow these foundation stones: that mental activity of the organism begins in sensorimotor processes which tend to use the environmental possibilities for the satisfaction of needs; that, from the beginning, things are vaguely sensed as objects standing out from a background; and that, furthermore, what objects are noted or what is seen will be determined by present needs and past experiences.

At this point an idea has been introduced which must be noted because all our further discussions rest upon it. It is said that past experience modifies the behavior of the present organism. Memory appears, then, to be functionally present from the beginning. Learning is possible by way of memory of preceding experience, which memory becomes a part of the present experience. For our purposes —that is, for a psychology upon which to base rational therapy—it is important to grasp the implications that a baby from the beginning remembers and learns from his experiences. The earliest relationships of the baby with its caretaker, usually its mother, are remembered, so that they influence the baby's behavior as a person in relation to another person or, primitively, the behavior of the baby as a body in relation to another body. The fact that ordinarily preverbal experiences cannot be verbally recalled does not deny the fact that they do modify subsequent behavior.

This matter of the effect upon a baby of its experiences in its earliest months is important for the theory of schizophrenia. What is implied is that physical experiences, long before the baby has any idea of self and mother as two separate persons, do modify behavior at the very primitive level of vegetative functions having to do with growth and development of structure and function of glandular and central nervous systems. The later functional capacity to adjust and to maintain integration may well be based upon the earlier conditions of growth. These involve the activity of the mother in so far as it promotes or interferes with the healthy development of her child.

There is implied that the infantile organism operates not only as a collection of part functions but as an entity, however vaguely defined. In addition to the sum of all its cells and their physiological interaction, there is the baby as a whole; this baby as a whole responds to the objects which stand out in its environment and to the changes which occur within its own economy. In order to have a word for the infant who so functions, a word for its over-all, its global, operation, we may call this concept of function its "primitive ego," or, if you like, the "anlage" of its ego. The ego, according to Freud (and undoubtedly it is true), is a body ego. In earliest infancy the body is not fully developed or differentiated as to function; that which is not differentiated cannot very well be integrated. So it is with the body ego: its functions are neither developed nor differentiated; it is diffuse; it is a sort of sensorimotor continuum, including memory, which experiences various sensorimotor—and, we might add, secretory—events. Some of these are useful, nay, vital, and some are damaging; all are likely to be repetitive. There emerges some patterning of experiences into those to be sought and those to be avoided, patterns involving various systems within the organism. These systems develop and overlap and eventually become integrated into an entity; this entity, the ego, of course varies from time to time in its extent and in the firmness of its integration. It might be said that its boundaries and its cohesiveness are altered—for example, in states of more asleepness or more awakeness—but its distinguishing characteristic is that it is a cohesive continuum.

The experiences through which the infantile ego goes are impressed upon it. They persist as memories and modifications of behavior; at the moment of the impression the experience is felt not only as a sensation but as an emotion. Might it be said that the emotion is how the infant feels when subjected to the patterns of sensations involved in the experience? These patterns include visceral and kinesthetic experiences. Emotion is part of an experience, and, in the sense that it enters into the processes which modify subsequent behavior, it is remembered.

The fleeting, transient instances of emotionally colored experience of infancy are repeated in various sensorimotor environmental combinations. They become interrelated and loosely organized.

The sequences through which emerges an infantile ego perceiving and reacting to environmental stimuli sources and those sequences through which emerges an infantile self, feeling as a whole about the whole situation, have been described as if they were separate processes. Of course, I do not think that there are actually two parallel but separate sets of sequences. It is merely a convenience in our clarification of our understanding to dissect that which is an entity, which may be considered objectively as ego, subjectively as self. It is necessary to keep in mind that the living baby is not dissected, nor should it be split up and forced to dissociate its self-feeling from its activities.

The infantile ego sleeps most of the time. Sleep is interrupted by experiences of cold, hunger, fear of loud noises, bright lights, and pain. Various patterns are learned —those of feeding, elimination, being bathed, being cuddled, and so forth. Now, although we speak of an ego and a self, we need to keep in mind how primitive the infant is. There is no verbal experience; there are no verbal symbols. Thinking and feeling are in terms of concrete experiences or images of them. Objects are not yet defined objectively, definitely; mother is not an entity including all her characteristics. The baby is not able to think of itself as an entity.

I suppose that, if we felt as does such a baby, we would describe ourselves as comfortable generally and as periodically persecuted; we would describe ourselves as anxious, angry, and helpless when persecuted. The persecution, as an experience of being persecuted, is, of course, all within the child. The bad, painful experience is within, be it hunger, colic, erupting teeth, cold, or mother's angry voice; all of it is felt within the child. There is no awareness that there is any external world. The infant's ego includes all the experiences of which it is capable.

If it is now assumed that this hypothetical, normal baby has arrived at this stage in its development in which an ego and a self, preoccupied with survival and the comfort which denotes security, are about to emerge as such, it will also be seen that this ego cannot go much further in the direction of differentiation and integration until it takes a great step toward reality. This step is the first of at least three which the infant will make. They have in common the meaning that the ego and the feeling of self withdraw from something which thereafter is felt and thought of as outside, external, to the ego and the self.

The practical necessity for the first withdrawal lies in the nature of things: the infant is not its mother, and vice versa. Unless this fact is admitted, the ego will continue to fail in all its efforts to deal with mother and her influence upon it. It will resort to magic, and the magic will not work. This may well be a critical point for the beginning of healthy or schizophrenic living.

This first withdrawal of the ego, felt as self, from mother comes about, we are taught, when the child is in need and mother fails at first to respond to the magical signal call, but later she does come. The child accomplishes the thought "this is the thing I needed"; its feeling about the thing is probably mixed—anger at the frustration and joy at its termination, at the return of comfort. It would seem that by this feat of the intellect the child sorts out what is cohesive and continuous experience of self from what is relatively intermittent and varied experience of mother. There must be a further emotional experience at this time. Although it is now possible to begin to think about how to control mother and to avoid feelings of persecution, neglect, and so forth, it is surely a sad thing, indeed, to realize that never again will you be the totality of the universe of your experience. The recent past, in which ego included mother, must seem like a paradise lost. Indeed, there is a theory propounded by persons, all of whom were once infants, that in those days they felt omnipotent. Obviously, this is a fiction. Comfortable, content, complete, satisfied, and secure they may have felt, but not omnipotent. Things just happened as they should, or sometimes they did not. There could be no question at all of power until the child had experienced frustration. When it had overcome this by some exertion, there was a sense of power. Until the child had learned of the relatively greater powers that there are in the world, it could not arrive at a speculation concerning its own omnipotence. This much, however, may be said: many of us have the sense that things once long ago were good. This is so strong in us that we still measure the present by comparison with the golden days of infancy.

As a result of this step which the infant has taken, his world now consists of self-ego and other than self—the human environment. In this account of the events which precede and lead into this situation, in which it may be believed that the baby perceives, however dimly, a certain continuum of experience felt as that of self and recognizes, however reluctantly, the existence of experiences involving another self, it needs to be repeated that the baby thinks only in very concrete and literal instances— pictures, sensory experiences, and such. Also, it ·should be recognized that all the baby's experiences are inner experiences. Now the question arises how the baby can sort out of its inner experiences those which are of self and those which are of that other self called "Mama." To attempt to find an answer to this question, we may, for the moment, refer to our adult, current experiences. As these words are written, the author has a sense of himself, of his present state of being, of his intentions and his activities, such as making marks upon paper. He is aware, also, of an activity he would call thinking.

This thinking goes, in part, something like this: students are remembered, that is, they are felt as presences in the writer's mind; it is believed that they actually existed as selves entirely outside myself, and it is known that these students are not actually in my mind. There occurs a generalization that there are other young student psychiatrists unknown to me but really existing somewhere. They are thought to be a good bit like those students already known, so they appear as presences in my mind—presences, of course, having the characteristics of the students I have known. Here am I writing for readers I do not know, who yet have a psychic reality for me. If I have correctly judged the situation, these readers do exist and may actually read these words; if I have not, they will not. To return to my babyhood, there was a time when I had experiences of the presence of my mother. Sometimes I was able to convince myself that she was actually present; she often helped in this conviction. Again, I had to admit that I had only an image or memory or sense of her presence when she was not actually at hand. We could say that the baby's discovery of the reality of its mother as a person is actually an intrapsychic process of sorting out what stimulus comes from outside and what is only a mental operation with symbols, remembered experiences, representing the real mother.

To recapitulate, all experience is originally that of the

self. Gradually the self sorts out all its experiences into those which correspond to external events and those which are intrapsychic operations with symbols. In the course of the acquisition of this skill, it is apparent that the baby has, as it were, drawn a boundary line. Originally all was self; now self has withdrawn from certain experiences and assigned them an outer significance, which, for the purposes of thought, can be symbolically duplicated within the boundaries of the self or the ego.

It is a necessary concomitant of the process of assigning external reality value to things and persons, and psychic reality to experiences of symbolic representations of these, that there emerges an entity, a self, who has a sense of being and usually a qualifying sense of being content or discontent, well or ill, pleased or angry, and so on. Healthy persons, and many others, are so used to the sense of self that they take it for granted and note only the changes in quality of affect or emotion, pain or comfort. Indeed, even psychoanalytic research preoccupied itself with the unconscious for a long time before it became possible to investigate the conscious ego itself, and this research is by no means yet complete.

Now, if it is tentatively agreed that a baby has arrived at consciousness of itself and of the existence in the environment of another human, it is in order to speculate how this baby can learn anything useful about the mother as another person, a motivated living organism, experiencing emotional states related to the baby. How can the baby differentiate her from inanimate things? How can it anticipate her motivations and emotions?

That a baby does so is undeniable. The question is only how it accomplishes the fact. To find an acceptable answer will require that we observe the baby with its mother and, since it is nonverbal, that we imagine from our observations how it feels and is motivated. We have by this maneuver removed our question from the baby to ourselves. How can we imagine how any human feels? By this introduction of understanding by analogy, we have admitted a possible source of error in that we may credit the baby with a fund of information and experience which we have available but which is not yet the baby's. There is, moreover, the possibility of a more serious error in that we may deny to the baby any skills or sources of information which have been repressed and are not available to us.

With these probable errors to be discounted, we may still try out our assumption that the baby and the psychiatrist do, in fact, learn something of the inner experience of another person, and by quite similar methods. We might call it the "scientific method," in that it begins with observations, the collection of data, and proceeds by setting up within the mind a symbolic equivalent of things as they seem. With this symbolic representation we can perform various mental operations of fantasy, imagination, make-believe situations and actions. And we can arrive at some hypothesis concerning the feelings, experiences, and expected behavior of our psychic presence of that person. We can then experiment, according to hypothesis, with the external person; we can compare our results with our expectations, correct our hypothesis, and finally achieve some degree of subjective certainty that our other person is possessed of predictable characteristic tendencies and behavior patterns. We come to know that certain facial expressions, tones of voice, and muscular tensions which we note in the other person and which make us feel angry or afraid do, in fact, mean that the other person is angry. Is there any good reason for us to deny that the baby, in its way, is a practical scientist?

To begin with, it must be said that, if the baby is a scientist, it works with data different from ours. It is limited, we suppose, to the concrete experiences, unable to generalize logically or to verbalize concepts. But it has at its command an instrument which, although many adults deliberately try to exploit it, most of them have forgotten. The instrument referred to has been called "resonance" or "empathy." Many believe, for example, that dogs possess this tool of investigation, that they can smell fear and can even share in the grief of their master; and there is abundant evidence in mob action of the contagion of hate, fear, guilt, and even courage. However it is done—that is, by way of what physical senses—babies do react to maternal acute emotion and also to chronic maternal states, phobic, compulsive, depressive, and so on. Resonance implies that the child, or the adult for that matter, does feel what is felt by another person to whom he is affectively related. By "to whom he is affectively related," we mean from whom he expects to derive some supplies needed for his security. The sensitiveness of a good diagnostician to the unconscious fury, fear, lust, or tension of a patient is probably not magical nor entirely perceptive-intellectual. The diagnostician may resort to the technique of consulting his own visceral responses, by which his diagnosis is in part made. This is nearly the same thing which the psychiatrist did as a baby when he was learning how his mother felt.

The recognition, correctly or incorrectly, of the state of being of the other person implies in infancy two processes. One is that of setting up within one's self the presence of the other person to see how he feels in you; the other is that of imputing to the other person one's own feelings and intentions and observing whether he acts appropriately. By these two processes of internalizing and externalizing, one comes to believe in a certain identity of himself with the other one, at least as to feelings and motives—often, also, as to appearances, abilities, beliefs, and prospects in life. There are degrees of this identification ranging from an actual belief that two are one, so that what happens to one is known and happens to the other, all the way to a mere sense that in a limited fashion the two have somewhat similar experiences in similar situations.

Identification as experienced in infancy is so realistically felt that as the infant grows older it is sensed as a cramping and inhibiting limitation of the infant's own self-sufficiency. He becomes interested in dissimilarities and in denying the identification. A boy of three tells his mother after dinner that she and her daughter can wash the dishes, while "we men," father and son, watch television. He is identifying with his father, but he is differentiating from his mother and sister.

But, having withdrawn its self-investment from the mother, the child is required by its need of her to return to her and to try again to include her in the self—at least to invest her with the quality of self to the extent that she is regarded as "mine." The processes here described are, of course, repeated many times in various situations. Separation and differentiation can be, and are, reversed under stress into fusion and denial of differences. Witness almost any baby who has acquired considerable independent feeling and who then has, let us say, got the measles or fallen on its nose. The baby forgets its development and regresses to helpless need for unity with the mother.

It is inevitable that confusion persists even after the separation. This is owing in part to the fact that mother plays a dual role in relationship to the child: she gives it satisfying care, but she also deprives it of accustomed comforts; she plays with, praises, and loves it, yet she also warns, scolds, and punishes it. In fact, the mother is sensed by the infant as of varying mood and performance. She is experienced as anywhere from absolutely good to relatively good to pretty bad to maliciously destructive. It is part of mature ego functioning to be able to tolerate and cope with the shifting valuations of another, be it wife, friend, child, or who not. But an infant has no such tolerance of its mother; to it she remains confusing. One of the duties of the ego is to avoid intolerable confusion, with its concomitant anxiety and paralysis of appropriate thought and action.

There is a delightfully simple technique by which the child may get momentary relief from the confusion created by a complexly functioning mother. The child, having no very firm hold on objective reality and no solidly cemented integration of its feelings, quietly denies that one mother does two series of things. It feels that there are two mothers, one good and one bad; likewise there are two babies, one good and one bad. This device resolves ambivalence and confusion, but in so doing it denies the bitter fact that there is no absolutely good or permanent mother-baby organism. This denial can be maintained only by persistent refusal to test it or to test reality or to admit contrary evidence. The cost of this device is arrest of further differentiation and of further gain in knowledge of reality and its resources for the welfare of the child.

This impasse can be resolved by a splitting of the ego or, to keep the terms used in describing the emergence of a sense of the existence of a self and a nonself, by withdrawal of the self from a part of itself. That which withdraws from the infantile ego and sets up a barrier to prevent confusion and to permit further development is the part known in the adult as his "ego," his conscious self. The extruded and denied infantile self, with its intense attachment to the mother, is left behind and denied participation in the further maturing of the ego; it is forgotten. Forgetting is an activity denying the act of remembering. We do not remember our early preverbal experiences. We operate only with such conscious drives from the past as we can translate into currently acceptable substitutes.

What is being discussed here is a splitting of the original infantile ego into two parts. One will go on developing its function in relation to reality; it will be, roughly speaking, the conscious self or will be able, more or less readily, to become conscious self and its content of symbols with which to think. The other will no longer be felt as self or acknowledged by the ego, which withdraws from it and sets up a barrier of repression against it. This dissociated, denied, and forgotten part may be called the "id." This id will be banished, but it will live, and its needs and drives will be forever seeking access to the ego that they may be satisfied. These drives have for their object the breast of the mother and those other experiences of her which have given comfort or caused anger.

So complete is the separation of the ego from the id that to the ego it seems that the id is unorganized, has no object, seeks only pleasure, is infantile in its aims, and learns nothing from experience of reality. In short, the id is so isolated that it cannot express or implement its intentions toward the object body of mother, or any substitute therefor, except by such disguises and displacements as are acceptable to the ego. Those which are acceptable are sensed by the ego as "mine" and are not recognized as coming from the id; therefore, the id itself is not recognized. The foregoing view of the id was presented to the psychoanalytic world in 1941 by Fairbairn.[1] Its general acceptance by analysts was not enthusiastic, yet it is vastly superior to the older concept of the id as actually objectless and structureless, particularly when the concepts are applied to clinical observations of schizophrenics. In these patients the id occasionally erupts, and one can see, as never in psychoneurotic patients, that it does have an object. Having seen this arrangement of relations between id and ego in schizophrenic patients, it becomes possible to see that it also fits the facts of psychoneurotic pathology.

According to this view, the "id" is a name for that very early ego state in which boundaries are not definite, objects—such as the maternal breast—not yet certainly excluded from the self, and the inevitable fact of frustration not met by any reaction other than fear and rage and denial. It becomes possible in this way to think consistently of the continuum of experience, which always involves some object or some image or presence or fantasy of an object. In order to cope with frustration and confusion, the continuing self, with its forward movement toward integration and interrelation with others, elects to put aside some of itself with its regressive insistence upon the good old days, the oceanic feeling of infancy.

It is demonstrable that part of the psyche does function as Freud has described it under the name of "id," per-

1. W. R. D. Fairbairn, "A Revised Psychopathology of the Psychoses and Psychoneuroses," *International Journal of Psychoanalysis,* Vol. XXII (1941), Parts 3 and 4.

sistently trying to achieve infantile goals. This part, as such, never gives up, never grows up, and never learns anything. It cannot learn, for, if anything is learned and translated into acceptable reality, it becomes the property of the conscious ego. The id, then, in any case, is seen as a power influencing the ego, sending messages to it which must be accepted or rejected; the id must be excluded, kept in repression, or be admitted only in such potency and terms as can be manipulated by the ego. The alternative is psychotic confusion. It should be noted here that the conception of the id which is presented by Fairbairn and with which I agree shows it to be a force driving always toward others. In that sense it is a force driving the child, the infant, to become a realistic human being capable of relationships with other human beings as such. This force is mediated and directed by the ego.

The conscious ego preserves a sense of adequacy in its ability to function coherently only by means of its techniques for exclusion of that excessive experience which would flood it with contradictory emotions and impulses. As for the guarded frontiers against objective reality, we can easily demonstrate the physiological protection against sensory bombardment. The eye not only receives light; it also excludes light, and, if the iris fails to exclude undue brilliance, the retina becomes blind to the stimulus. The ear hears only within a limited range of tone; it goes deaf to the long-continued stimulus of a constant pitch. Although less easily demonstrated, it is a fact that each of us can verify that the conscious ego can ignore stimuli which have entered the barrier. For example, a child or a psychoanalytic patient may fail to respond to spoken instructions or comments. He may even deny that he understood them and may ask what was said. However, not infrequently, if asked what he thinks may have been said, he can repeat it correctly. He may now go one step further in his denial of the stimulus and act as if the statement had been heard in its opposite or negative form. So we see that there is defense in depth against having to react to the actions of the persons in the environment.

The boundaries which the ego in health erects against the infantile ego or id are more difficult to observe. Psychoanalytic research has convincingly proved to those who have been analyzed that there is active in their psyche much of which they are not aware. A healthy person awake and alert has no evidence directly of the existence of his id. But this same person spends about a third of his time asleep—he dreams. Occasionally his dreams are terrifying, and he awakes to the realization that there are in his sleeping mind presences of great value and potency. However, as he thinks about his dream, it usually recedes. Its more bizarre and eerie features grow dim, and he is able to report some sort of rationalized explanation—even that it was the lobster he ate for dinner which made him dream of catastrophic episodes. Fortunately, there are also dreams which are much more to his liking. Having puzzled long and fruitlessly over an idea and given up its solution, he may have some night, out of nowhere, a dream of a resolution of his puzzle. So we see that from beyond the usual boundaries of the self there comes evidence of powerful destructive and constructive tendencies. And, apart from dreams, healthy persons may observe that something goes on which eludes their consciousness. We have our slips of the tongue and pen. (A young minister wrote to a friend that on the night before his wedding he dreamed he had several children; he added that he guessed this was a "wish fillfulment." Need it be added that the following night he was impotent?) We all have our accidents, our failures of memory, various repetitive, apparently useless, or harmful preoccupations.

That which has been excluded by the ego from itself in order that the ego might further develop and differentiate in its interchange with the real environment is defended against by a barrier which permits return of only such impulses and feelings as can be managed without danger of disintegration of the self. It is, in large part, the infantile interest in its own comfort and security in terms of physiological needs. The separation of ego from id has occurred by the time the mother appears as a person rather than a breast, and certainly by the time the infant begins to make some meaning out of the mother's words addressed to it. It is important to recognize that up to this point all the baby's interests are self-centered; although it reacts to maternal emotion, its reactions are for its own security, not for her pleasure. After verbal communication has begun to be meaningful and the child has come to think that mother has emotions like its own, it is possible—indeed necessary—that her feelings be considered and that something be done to modify her moods and impulses. Whereas heretofore the baby may have stopped reaching for forbidden things because of fear of being slapped or hurt, it now is able to attempt to restrain itself for the purpose of pleasing her, of winning her approval. She has become a person in the eyes of the baby.

This person, or mama, is bigger, stronger, wiser, and more powerful than the baby. Comparable to Superman, she is Superego. She is feared, loved, held in awe and envy and hate. To her are attributed, of course magnified, attributes similar to those of the baby. For example, she is hungry as is the baby. As a notion emerges that eating leads to increased size, it is obvious to the baby that the large mama eats a great deal; as the baby is hungry for her, so it is possible that she might eat the baby; nor is the idea entirely mistaken. Mothers have eaten their children not so long ago or so far from here. And, as the child in anger defecates just to plague its mother, it is not inconceivable to it that she might flush it down the toilet; in fact, it has been wanting to do just that to the new baby but has refrained from fear of retaliation.

These fantasies are terrifying when the child believes them—they make it draw away from the mother. But it has to have her help in eating, defecating, and everything it does. The old device which helped it to keep fairly calm in the face of disrupting danger, which separated it from the vast outside, was again invoked to separate the id from the self. It placed the mother-baby symbiotic unity outside the self, so that the self could further realize itself. Now, in the presence of the dangerous mother, the angry, destructive, depriving, disciplinary, threatening mother, the child can again set her up within itself as a presence and then separate, or dissociate, or repress this part of itself with its included presence of her.

This leaves baby and the real external mother in a relatively simplified relationship which the baby can attempt to manipulate. It can experimentally test out the situation with a symbol—the superego—in its mind. It can then apply the results of its experiments to its actual mother. For most children this method of learning how to do what is expected and how not to do what is forbidden works pretty well. Very few children are killed or tortured to death by their mothers.

One is impressed by the restless, relentless cruelty of the bad and destructive mother-presence, which seems to us to be very much more savage than the actual mother, unfortunate as are some of the punishments she devises. Similarly, one is shocked by the cruelty of little children, and new parents are surprised that children like, and demand, to hear stories of "Little Red Riding Hood" and of all the murderers who are found in other tales for children. It becomes apparent that, as the child takes into itself the impressions of the punitive mother, it endows her with its own primitive impulses. From somewhere in its animal nature, perhaps from inherited readiness to think in terms of the experience of the race, the child has ability to think in terms of the most primitive justice, such as the talion law, which we have in the formulas "an eye for an eye and a tooth for a tooth," "let the punishment fit the crime," "if thy right hand offend thee cut it off." These are expressions which have literal and terrible meaning for children, and, when mother says to the baby after its bath, "I could eat you up" and proceeds to kiss the baby's belly or bottom, the child believes her. If we follow this child into its later years, we may find that—if it be organized upon the hysterical pattern—it may continue to desire and fear fellatio and that this fear covers an actual fear of being bitten. If in later years the child is more schizophrenic, we may find that this fear of being eaten up is a component of the primary genital phobia.

In order to carry on the business of living, of experimenting with new experiences, of investigating everything, of practicing skills in locomotion, speaking, and manipulating things, one needs to be at ease, relaxed, co-ordinated, free to imagine and act; hence one has to repress, dissociate, and deny this terrible presence of the destroying mother and with it that part of the self which stands guard over it. There must be supported a barrier which would keep out excesses of danger which would paralyze the child, yet there must be some traffic across the barrier so that the childish ego can sufficiently frighten itself to control its impulses to the extent that the objective mother will not act like the terrible superego avenger. Such traffic persists to an extent in most persons; fears of God or of the devil or of witches or of policemen or of tax collectors or of one's husband or wife or of public opinion seem to be among the visible representations of this buried childish fear of the mother.

I have now described what I find is a useful idea of the process of becoming a person in terms which imply three separate splits of the ego. The first is one between itself and the mother; then there occurs one between self and those impulses and desires which deny the separateness of the mother, which is thought of as the withdrawal of the self from its id; and then there is a further separation between the self and that part of itself which includes an animistic, savage, punishing, primitive, and avenging impression of mother which is called "superego." There emerges, in this reconstruction, an ego which functions more or less consciously and which exists in a real world of external objects and persons and also in close, but repressed, relationship to that part of itself which fights the punitive lawgiver and that part which seeks the potentially all-satisfying maternal breast. This ego experiences its own imagery; some of it is regarded as imagination, dream, make-believe, planning, thinking, and so forth. None of it is felt as id or superego in a healthy person. Only in illness does the id or superego invade the ego, and it then is experienced as if it had real objective or external existence. Passing note may be taken of the figures of speech which one hears occasionally from persons who are in the course of analysis. They comment that their id or their superego has done this or that; this, of course, is never quite true if they are not psychotic. It is a superficial, witty evasion of responsibility for an act of the ego in guilty co-operation with the id or the superego.

The most acutely conscious activity of the ego is related to problems, to new situations requiring concentrated attention. Capable of being conscious, yet not actually so, is a vast content of attitudes, beliefs, preferences, prejudices, fears, dislikes, desires, and so on, which have their being in that they are residues of experience. It is most impressive that much of our firm belief rests upon no actual evidence and cannot be factually proved. Where it comes from is easy to guess. It was taught by that person, or those persons, from whom we derived our sense of human likeness. As a single, personal example, the writer remembers experiencing a shock when in Hungary he was repeatedly told that all the Swiss people are crazy. This he angrily denied and, as proof, offered his opinions concerning Hungarians, of whom he had known a few for a few months. (Unwittingly he thereby documented their belief in "crazy Americans.") Why his conviction that the Swiss are exceptionally fine people? His mother and grandmother had told him of his grandfather, who was Swiss; the grandfather was dead, but the tales about him were alive. What made it so serious was that he was said to be just like his grandfather. Upon no better evidence, he believed the Swiss to be a superior nation of morally, intellectually, physically wonderful persons. But the Hungarians had no Swiss grandfathers, dead or alive. Perhaps even they were not objective, for they were involved in black-market money transactions with the Swiss. What is important to sense about a person is that he is conscious of his beliefs and ideals, but he is not conscious of their origin or of the existence within himself of a presence whose vengeance he fears, were he to deny these beliefs.

The foregoing example is a personal one of strong conviction without any rational or scientific evidence. As such, it may serve to illustrate a rather vast area of belief, faith, fear, hate, superstition, and so on, to be found in nearly any "normal" person's mind, present there without any adequate experiential or experimental data. Not only is this collection of notions present; it is persistent and insistent, it participates largely in the government of the life of the believer, and it is not readily responsive to contrary evidence. So it is said by many quiet-loving persons that it is best not to discuss religion, politics, and so forth with contrary-minded persons. The question arises why most persons entertain and value so tenaciously their prejudices against all the rational evidence. An answer is suggested in the thought that what is so vigorously defended, so overvalued, so impervious to modification by virtue of new experience, is most likely to have its origin in early childhood interchange with the person or persons to whom the child looked for its support and security of life and relief of discomfort.

Of course, these attitudes and opinions, with their great affective charge, which were taken into the young ego from the collection of such prejudices held by the parent are not by any means immovably fixed in either mind or heart. Very many of us have departed far from our infantile training and inculcated beliefs; education or modification of ideas and attitudes is not impossible. All psychotherapy is based upon this fact. In truth, it is very easy under certain conditions to change one's mind. Among these conditions are, prominently, two, which are related. One is that the teacher or modifier be a person who has prestige in the eyes of the student. This pre-eminent authority may stem from the commonly agreed-upon high standing of the person, but it is enormously reinforced if the teacher also reminds the student of a parent who in childhood was admired, envied, and regarded as favorable to the child. The other condition under which a youth readily learns modification or reversal of his opinions is that in which his new ideas come to him from a contemporary best friend or from a contemporary group or gang to which he feels it is a distinction to belong. Given intellectual ability, it is easier to accept rationally demonstrable new truth than a merely different set of prejudices, but we dare not underestimate the often-decisive potency of beliefs and customs coming to a person from a person or group representing the all-powerful parent of childhood.

There is an apparent contradiction in the statement that you, a normal person, who believed, let us say, in miracles because your mother believed in them and sent you to Sunday school, where everyone believed, are now a firm believer in the law of cause and effect, the orderly sequence of events according to the laws of physics, chemistry, and biology, because your professors and classmates in medical school had prestige derived from your desire to believe your mother and father and taught you an opposing code of belief by virtue of the analogous position they held in your estimation to that which your parents once had. But so it seems to be.

What I am talking about is no less than the tremendous potency of the superego in directing, by way of approval or disapproval, the thinking and feeling you do. And now, having said that current substitutes for infantile caretakers can alter and revise the teaching of their predecessors, it is necessary to record that there are many relapses from newly gained objectivity. For example, there was a young surgeon who had been brought up in a fundamentalist family. But between the ages of fourteen and seventeen the events of his life were such that he revolted and turned altogether toward science, biology, and surgery as a career. At best he was agnostic; at his loudest he embraced atheism. And so he went along among colleagues of similar materialistic and realistic orientation. Then, one day in his early thirties, he found himself in a situation requiring, so it seemed to him, that he perform an operation upon one of his children. Why not? Free of superstition and silly sentiment, why not? So he did. But, when the child fought the anesthetic noisily, this so very rational surgeon heard himself promising God that he would not swear any more, he would not smoke again, and so on, if only the child lived. This was at 10:00 A.M., and not till 3:00 P.M. did he smoke. There, in all its original power, was the religious belief of childhood, the asking for a miracle, the promising of what, had he kept his word, would indeed have been a miracle.

It becomes evident, if we observe ourselves, that we live not only our own lives, perform not alone our own mental operations, but persistently and repetitively think, feel, and act as if our parent were alive and in control within our own bodies. This state of things is unavoidably one of conflict, which the ego tends to fear and to avoid. So it is necessary, daily, even in adult years, to keep up barriers between those thoughts, feelings, and actions which would conflict, expressing some and ignoring others, playing now one role, now another.

The foregoing statement is generally true in that most of us are somewhat neurotic or immature. But it appears also to be true that one may, in the process of growing up, assimilate into himself as his own belief and ideal and code of ethics much which was originally the point of view of his superego. In so far as this is done, one frees himself from the need for and fear of his parental presences in his mind. This is one of the hoped-for accomplishments of psychoanalysis.

What is unique in the person is a certain continuum, which, to be maintained, requires that we both separate the ego from its punitive and its desired parental presences and arrange for a persisting close relationship with these same presences. This, in part, throws a light upon the inconsistencies and absurdities to which we are all given.

There is a great deal more involved in becoming and

being a person than is indicated in this account. However, this great deal more can, in large part, be fitted into this frame of reference.

Having attempted a formulation of the processes involved in becoming a normal person, it is now in order to look for such differences in process as may occur with some regularity in the course of becoming a schizophrenic person. To record observations of these differences will require special and emphatic reference to the mothers of schizophrenics. I will, therefore, precede my comments upon the vicissitudes in the development of the schizophrenic ego by some remarks about the mothers of schizophrenics.

CHAPTER VI

The Mothers of Schizophrenics

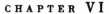

Any illuminating acquaintance with a schizophrenic as a human being in a human environment—that is, as a creature endeavoring in some fashion to exist within the framework of human relatedness—tends to reveal that his peculiar schizophrenic problems and presuppositions, interests, and interdictions derive their peculiarity primarily from his attitudes toward his mother. These attitudes are the precipitate—one might almost say the structured residue—of his experience of her. To appreciate him in his futile dilemma of dependence-independence, it is necessary to learn what these experiences have meant to him. His experiences are his subjective impressions of and responses to his mother rather than what she objectively does to him. The experiences are revealed in his memories, meanings, values, and beliefs concerning her and her substitutes and also concerning himself in relation to her. We would seek to learn in what sense he is still endeavoring to establish rapport with her, while simultaneously struggling to free himself from what he feels are her demands and interdictions.

It appears upon exploration that she—the mother—is a presence within the schizophrenic's ego and is to him a real, living, inescapable problem of relationship. This may be true, unfortunately, after her actual death. One learns something about this presence from what he says about her and about women and persons in general and about himself as he sees himself through her eyes. What he does not, and dares not, say about her is equally revealing. For example, a schizophrenic youth attributed his collapse to masturbation now given up but evident to him as the cause of the rather full veins upon the backs of his hands. He thought his mother had recognized this sign of his degeneracy and had, upon this evidence, hospitalized him. Now it happened that she also had full veins on her hands. A would-be clever psychiatrist drove this patient, through much resistance, to a logical conclusion: if his mother knew that his veins were due to masturbation, and she also had such veins, then hers were also due to masturbation. The result of this stroke of genius was, among other things, that the patient got his mother to take him out of the hospital, back to her.

Fortunately for us in our search for information, however unfortunate it may be for the schizophrenic patient, we do have this further source of data on the mother's attitudes. Despite what he says or holds in silence or denies about her, she is a presence internalized within the patient. This presence modifies what he feels and thinks and does. As a result of the modification, he unwittingly reveals his conception of his mother's unconscious fantasies, expectations, and fears. His own behavior reveals to us an otherwise hidden aspect of his mother's attitude toward him and herself.

Perhaps it needs to be said that this portrayal of mother cannot be accepted as a simple and real photograph of her preconscious preoccupations. It is, of course, retouched, so that in one light it ennobles and glorifies and purifies her into a divinity, and in another light it caricatures her weaknesses, foibles, and pretenses with an energy that can only be understood as an expression of vengeful resentment. It should be repeated here that the patient, of course, has also added to the attributes of the mother contributions from his own infantile impulses which he has ceded over to her, so that she appears more infantile in the form of her presence than she does in reality.

A further check upon the patient's portrayal of his mother is available and is probably more valid and important for therapeutic use. It is the interaction before our eyes between the mother and her child. We see her letters to him and her visits to him, and we cannot avoid seeing his reactions in anticipation of, during, and after her interventions in his hospitalization. Nowhere else is it more evident how painful it is to be schizophrenic than in the patient's encounters, while acutely ill, with his mother.

After these encounters patients have often remarked that "she would be all right if only she were not my mother." Certainly we may observe that my awareness of my mother and your awareness of yours are very different things from your awareness of my mother and mine of yours. This is probably more significantly true for schizophrenics than it is for us. So our further efforts to understand the bondage of the schizophrenic to the presence of his mother leads us to compare his presentation of her with our own observations of her, with our experiences in dealing with her, and with what she can be persuaded to tell us of herself. We may also note what her other, nonschizophrenic children say about her. We may learn something of what sort of person she is, objectively observed by others than her schizophrenic child.

In spite of her recognized importance to the schizophrenic and her potency for good or bad in the outcome of his treatment and his illness, there are few objective, scientific studies of her in the literature. This lack of research into her nature may well be due to some reaction within psychiatrists against her. It may be not altogether unlike that of her schizophrenic child. It is expressed in the tendency to try to avoid and deny and withdraw from her lest we dissolve into unseemly rage against her. Psychiatrists certainly appear to need to fight some definitely bad feelings which they have toward the mothers of their schizophrenic patients.

At any rate, in the near-absence of scientific research, there is coming into our language an ugly term for the mother of the schizophrenic. She is coming to be called the "schizophrenogenic mother." This term is analogous to "pathogenic bacteria." The use of a term by analogy is a bad thing because it implies an etiologic value which is not proved. Nor would it be easy to set up an experiment which would prove it. Koch's postulate would be most difficult to apply. In the case of bacteria, effective pathogenicity requires a susceptible host. Your tubercle bacilli are not very successful in crippling you, whereas they might kill your neighbor or your child. So it is with the imputed schizophrenogenic mother. Her alleged pathogenic power wrecks the life of one of her children but does not have any demonstrated, devastating influence upon others of her children.

I think that this bit of name-calling without proof, and without much serious effort to prove it, is evidence of something within psychiatrists which may well interfere with their therapeutic orientation. The treatment of the schizophrenic is not so simple as the separation of him from his mother. In fact, an effort to carry out this simple isolating operation may be disastrous. I suspect, but cannot prove, that psychotherapists who are in sufficient resonance to work with schizophrenic patients are thereby aroused at very regressive levels to feel some of what must be the inevitable residue of resentment which any child must have felt toward the mother who was bringing him up. In any case, the fact is that "schizophrenogenic mother" is gaining currency as a term. This unscientific use of a scientific-sounding term is part of the evidence that psychiatrists do not generally like or have sympathy for or understand the mothers of schizophrenic patients.

To document the psychiatrist's attitude, let me report an experience of my own. In one phase of my state hospital service it was my duty to see the patients' relatives when they could not be dealt with adequately by the resident physician. This was work and one good reason for my escaping from the state hospital, yet it was also valuable experience. The mothers of schizophrenics made an impression unlike that made by any other relatives of patients. One clear point was that they did not use or hear words as conveying factual information. Words were instruments with which to maneuver or mislead the hearer; facts and real situations could be ignored and forgotten if only the right words were spoken. A typical interview began with superficial pleasantness, covering a wary disinclination to supply information. The request to take Jimmy home was made as if a long-suffering and tormented soul were merely asking for a drink of cool water and the doctor would, of course, provide relief. This attitude accented rather than hid the implied suspicion that the doctor was an arbitrary brute who would automatically refuse. The case of Jimmy would be discussed point by point; his mother would agree that she remembered that only a few weeks ago Jimmy broke up the furniture in his room and even threatened to attack her. She would appear to accept the facts that he was now in a disturbed ward, that he was mute and refusing to eat or drink, that he resisted toileting and bathing, and that he refused to see her. She would agree that Jimmy was a sick boy and needed specialized care and protection. Then her further words would convey appreciation for all that the hospital was doing for Jimmy and for the doctor's attention at this moment to her. It escaped me for some time that she had changed the subject. Her thanks were for my attention to her, not for that to Jimmy. This frequently seduced me into feeling that I had managed the interview successfully, and so I was startled by her next words. They were expressed hopefully, pleadingly, or threateningly and were, "Then I can take Jimmy home next week?" I would then feel obliged to review the pathetic list of reasons why Jimmy must stay with us some months, and she would agree with me again point by point. Then, gathering strength, she would launch into a speech to the effect that if she took Jimmy home now he would eat for her; those strange men on the ward made Jimmy sick; he never was any trouble at home; she always understood him. So it would go. Jimmy was not really sick; his mother could care for him best; the hospital made him crazy. She would conclude her speech with a tearful, desperate plea, rarely put bluntly but saying indirectly that mother herself was going to pieces, that she needed Jimmy at home where he belonged, with her, and that she could not get along without him. I must confess that my pity for these mothers usually won out over my anger at their impervious obstinacy. This does not mean that Jimmy was allowed to go home, but the idea was being implanted in my mind that these mothers were ill; they needed their sons and daughters to give them a reason for existence, and even a conviction that they did exist.

I am indebted to Dr. Will Elgin, of the Sheppard and Enoch Pratt Hospital, for another repeated observation which, because it is characteristic, needs reporting. For many years Dr. Elgin, in the process of admitting patients, observed the enactment of a scene which assumed diagnostic significance. His office arrangement permitted relatives a choice of three seats, one opposite his desk, one at the end of it quite near him, and one several feet away. He observed that when the mother and father of the patient appeared together to arrange admission, there occurred something of significance. If mother sat in one of the two chairs at his desk, and father sat off in a corner, it usually followed that mother took over the discussion, did the talking, made the arrangements, and even read the fine print on the contract. Father, meanwhile, looked unhappy and was silent save for an occasional abortive effort to modify certain of the mother's statements. When this was the course of the admission interview, he came to know that the odds were that the patient would be schizophrenic. There is an interesting addendum. In a later interview father, appearing alone, was often very aggressive in his criticism and his demands and accusations. However, it could often be demonstrated that his belligerence was that of a very unwilling agent of his wife.

These almost routine experiences with the mothers of schizophrenics suggest several possibilities. One is that their anxiety, guilt, and sense of incompetence are such that they can tolerate the situation only if they convince themselves that they are in command and if they take over and direct the conversation in an effort to keep it away from those subjects which they do not dare to discuss. Another is that these women are vain or, if you prefer, narcissistic and are actually more concerned with the impression which they are making of themselves than they are with the realities concerning the patient. It has been observed that many of the mothers of schizophrenic patients appear young for their age. They tend to dress younger than they are, and they are often quite susceptible to flattery concerning their appearance, particularly their youthfulness. One would gather, furthermore, that these women act in the manner in which they do partly because of their conscious and rationalized sense of their general superiority to men and to doctors and also, specifically, to anyone else when it comes to the care of their child. In large measure, their generally hostile attack against men and doctors reveals their fear of an accusing counterattack.

As previously stated, remarkably little has been systematically reported concerning the impression psychiatrists have gained concerning the mothers of schizophrenic patients. However, you may find some reported opinions. At one time it was generally felt that these mothers were unconditionally hostile and rejecting of their children and that any appearance to the contrary was a reaction formation—a superficial assertion of their own motherly goodness. It later came to be felt that many of these mothers were markedly ambivalent, impressively overprotective and also rejecting. This would seem to be nearer the fact. Perhaps a better statement of the situation would be that these mothers are devastatingly, possessively all-loving of their child who is to be schizophrenic. This love is idealized, romantic, and unrealistic and leads to extensive denial of anything they observe in the child contrary to their fantasies concerning him. The result is, of course, disastrous to the child, but it does not follow that the mother meant it to be so; she meant to destroy only what we would regard as the naturalness, the normal **badness**, the spontaneity, the investigative curiosity, the boldness of her child, so that she could keep it good and ideal and completely her own.

Put in another way, these mothers love their children who become schizophrenic not only excessively but conditionally. The condition for their love is one which the schizophrenic child cannot meet. If he does, to a degree, meet it, in so doing he sacrifices his realization of a personality of his own, independent of hers. This sacrifice is made, apparently, by observance of what I have been calling "interdictions," with the result that the patient has large blank spots—areas in which information is not assimilated and experience is not associated with the main theme of his life—so that he is narrow, naïve, and immature.

The notion which is still prevalent among psychiatrists that the mothers of schizophrenic patients are utterly hostile, malicious, and in every way a misfortune seems to grow out of the frustration of the doctors, frequently precipitated by mother's unfortunate interventions in the patient's care. Also, it seems that those doctors who have some success with schizophrenics are likely to be those who are capable of a good bit of identification with the patient. They are capable of absorbing, as it were, if not the patient's delusions, at least his affective attitude of hostility, suspicion, and futility in relation to his mother. This attitude, of course, on the part of the physician has not been profitable and does not seem in any case to be the whole truth. It is quite possible that the psychiatrist, like the patient, having arrived at an opinion concerning the mother—perhaps even before meeting her—proceeds to treat her in such a fashion as to provoke the very reactions for which he criticizes her.

It is certainly true that schizophrenic children, whatever may have been done to them by their mothers, often do a very good job of retaliation and of heartbreaking revenge. The almost irresistible impulse of the schizophrenic patient to return again and again to his mother, although he knows that possibly he will have a recurrence of acute disorder when he does so, might argue that he feels rejected or that he still feels the need of revenge. It might equally well argue that he still feels that there is hope of winning rapport and affection. More probably, it indicates marked ambivalence upon his part and upon hers.

Maternal ambivalence is an area in which there is contradictory evidence. A number of the mothers of schizophrenic patients have reported murderous intents toward their unborn children. Some have commented upon the fight which they must carry on against murderous impulses toward the nursing infant; and some of these mothers have actually been unable to care for their children, wishing the task upon grandmother or someone else. The mother of a schizophrenic girl, herself psychotic, tried to kill the girl by putting her in a gas oven when she was six months old. She tried again to asphyxiate the family when this girl was six years old. This mother killed herself when the daughter was eight years old, and the daughter killed herself when she was twenty-six. The mother died by running under a locomotive. The daughter inhaled ether and fell out of a window. It may be noted that she combined the inhalation of a gas and the crushing injury from a collision. It is this kind of evidence which leads to the idea that schizophrenic patients have never fully separated themselves from their mothers. It is not infrequent that mothers of schizophrenic patients say that they would rather see their children dead than have them hospitalized.

There is equally reliable evidence that many of the mothers of schizophrenics actually accepted their babies warmly and took excellent animal care of them while these babies were small and were not regarded as individuals having any will or wilfulness contrary to that of the mother. It is certain that the majority of mothers of schizophrenic patients have shown considerable moral sadism, insisting on extremely early habit training, and have somehow managed to squelch the normal fight which children exhibit. As a result each is able to report, almost uniformly, that the schizophrenic child was the best one she ever had, the easiest to care for, the most quickly trained, the cleanest, and, in short, nearly a perfect infant. Part of this reporting, regrettably, is the result of amnesia. One learns from the patient, and occasionally on acquaintance with the siblings or other members of the family one learns from them, that this delightfully good child had night terrors, was a thumb-sucker, nail-biter, bed-wetter, or sleepwalker or was given to temper tantrums. These are the things which apparently the mother must forget in order to keep her illusion concerning her child and herself. The denial of the baby's actual behavior is known sometimes to go so far that the child is not regarded as alive and human; it is felt to be a toy, a plaything, unreal and insensate.

Psychiatrists interviewing the mothers of schizophrenic patients have reported feeling much as a schizophrenic seems to feel—that mother is superficially optimistic, cooperative, friendly, and yielding, but that not far beneath the surface she freezes when anything unpleasant is mentioned. She holds one at arm's length, being quite critical, demanding, and long-suffering out loud. As a group, these mothers appear not as angry and rejecting women but as righteous persons, expecting no reward for their very good maternal attitude but extremely sensitive, hurt, and silently accusing all and sundry, including the patient, for their troubles. Of particular moment for our purpose is the observation that these mothers, when giving histories, making arrangements, and so forth, are quite literal-minded, taking statements at their face value, not generalizing, showing no depth. In short, in a mild form, they are showing a characteristic of the schizophrenic thinking difficulty.

If we summarize our impressions of the attitudes of these mothers toward their own parents, we may say that as a group they reported that they loved their fathers or felt that they had some love from them. But, on the whole, the fathers were weak, sometimes brutal, absent, and in one way or another quite inadequate and unreliable. Frequently also there was some feeling that the fathers were either somewhat abnormal heterosexually or were regarded as possibly homosexual. On the other hand, these mothers of schizophrenics nearly uniformly report their respect for their mothers. Almost without exception, they give the impression that they are saying not only that they respect their particular mothers but that through their mothers they have come to idealize motherhood—they believe in the divinity of maternity. This is not an uncommon idea in our culture, but one feels that these women are more desperately devoted to it than are the run of people. The maternal grandmothers of the patients are usually reported to have ruled their homes either directly or, more commonly, through tears and suffering. Mothers of the patients have learned this technique from these grandmothers and with very few exceptions dominate, in one way or another, the family situation, including the husband. Usually they employ the hurt techniques to make others feel guilty; much more rarely they are arbitrarily and angrily in charge. As for the relation to the children, these mothers, in addition to reporting them as model children, also most frequently remark that as little children the patients worshiped their mothers; they frequently comment that they still do.

What appears to be the fact is that these mothers saw only the normal, outer shell of the children and were impervious to any impressions as to what went on within them. This attitude is not limited to the children who are to become schizophrenic; in a way it is present in the descriptions that these women give of their husbands. When asked how and why they came to be married, these mothers sometimes give the superficial answer that they married for love. But, again, they seem factual and concrete and, as a rule, indicate that they married to get away from home and that they married particular men because they were gentlemen. This means that in courting them they made no sexual advances or demands. These women do not see any contradiction in their admiration of their mothers and their wish, as soon as possible, to get away from the mothers and establish homes of their own. Nor do they see any contradiction between the desire to get away from mother into one's own home and a need to establish one's own home within a stone's throw of the mother. These women have a way of describing their marriages as anything from good to perfect, and yet, when they are pinned down to details, it is found that these allegedly perfect marriages have been punctuated by separations, by bouts of alcoholism and unfaithfulness on the part of the husband, by brutality at times, and frequently have ended in divorce. The divorce rate in this group is high; particularly, the number of divorces due to incompatibility in the two persons because of mental illness is higher than would be found in general.

Returning to the attitudes of these mothers toward their sick children, it appears that few of these schizophrenic children were unwanted, as had been some of their siblings who fared much better in life. Also, having arrived, these schizophrenic children appear, none of them, to have been really the preferred children. At least in their own opinion, some other sibling was preferred, and many of these schizophrenic patients set about early in life seriously squelching their own personalities in order to produce an imitation of the envied sibling. It did not matter whether this sibling was of the same or of the other sex. This may be a factor in the high incidence of homosexual preoccupation in schizophrenic patients or, to put it more accurately, in their uncertainty as to their sex. Mothers frequently report that these patients were normal, popular, healthy children, but one learns that actually they succeeded in their enterprises through the mediation of their siblings and that their friends were the friends of the siblings and not of their own making.

It needs to be said explicitly that most of these mothers are described by the family as obsessively concerned about cleanliness. There are reports of much sterilizing of bottles, nipples, babies, and so forth. A few of the mothers report that they discontinued nursing because they found it pleasurable. A number of them discontinued because they did not want "breast babies," whatever that may mean, or they used some such euphemism as a reason for their discontinuance. On the whole, there is a suggestion that the earliest relationship of the baby to the mother was relatively good, quite satisfactory to both mother and child, at least in comparison with what followed. This is of particular theoretical interest as indicating that there is in the schizophrenic a basis in his early infantile experience for his persistent craving to return to the preobjective, and certainly preverbal, mother-child relationship. In proportion as the mothers were not intuitive and responsive, it would appear that the schizophrenic babies became exceptionally skilled at reacting to the conscious and unconscious attitudes, emotions, and fantasies of the mother. A great many schizophrenics seem to spend their lives living out some fantasy of the mother.

One conspicuous area in which this is demonstrated in later life is that in which the mother manages to encourage her daughter to seek the company of young men but always objects to any young man the girl could get or really seemed to like. Sometimes the mother competes openly for the young man's attention, thereby breaking up his interest in the daughter. The same pattern has been seen with mothers who tended to control and dominate their adolescent sons until the sons finally gave up interest in girls.

A final comment concerning the report which these mothers give of their relationships to their children, which tends to clinch the idea that they actually have no awareness of the reality of their children, is that the illness—the onset of the catastrophic condition—comes to the mother of the schizophrenic as a great surprise. She has not been aware up to that moment of the catatonic episode that her child was not happy, comfortable, or prosperous. True, she was overconcerned, ambitious, and interfering with his affairs in an effort to promote his interests. This was because she was such an exceptionally good mother rather than because the child was already conspicuously peculiar. Unfortunately, these mothers are not capable, as a rule, even after the patients have long been ill, of grasping the facts of the situation. They continue to be hopeful that their children will yet conform to their expectations.

A conspicuous example of this attitude was that of a mother whose son, to escape her, went to a university on the opposite fringe of the continent. As he approached graduation, his mother advised him that she had picked the girl for him to marry, had bought a lot upon which he could build a house, and had the promise of a job for him. He managed to sabotage all this by becoming acutely ill and failing to graduate. After some months in the hospital, when he was considered well enough to return to the community, his mother crossed the continent and greeted him with the information that she had picked out another girl for him and was about to get a job which he could take at once. As one might expect, he relapsed at this point.

It is a frequent experience that when a patient has managed to get himself put together so that he may leave the hospital and return home over a week end, he comes back reporting that everything was fine, he was treated wonderfully, it was nice to be home, the food was good, but somehow he began to feel worse. He suspects that he cannot live with his mother. This suspicion usually disappears after a time, and he again plans to return to his mother; or he may make elaborate plans to depart from her, but, as a preliminary step to doing so, he will go back

117

for one more visit. It is reminiscent of the way in which high-school students break off their love affairs.

Now, if we endeavor to reconstruct some of these observations that we have made from our experience of schizophrenic patients and their mothers, we can imagine what must have been the life-situations of the mothers. It would appear that they were dominated by their own mothers, who were opposed to sex and men and who were competitive both with husbands and with children for dominance in the household. They declined to grow old and let these children of theirs mature into motherhood. These mothers of schizophrenics, as a group, might be called "obsessive-compulsive." They are abnormally interested in cleanliness and propriety. They are idealists concerning marriage and love, although they seem to be quite vague about sexual matters. One would suspect that they are examples of Freud's observation that at the center of the obsessive structure there is an exquisite hysteria. It appears in getting the histories, with the questions about mother in mind, that the mother either was a frigid or was an immature person without capacity and tolerance for mature psychosexual intimacy with another person, or, if she had such capacity, for one reason or another it was in eclipse at the time of the patient's infancy.

In order to keep some perspective and an open mind concerning other points of view, it is necessary at this point to mention the fact that many observers regard schizophrenia as a condition made possible only by reason of some inherent defect in the infant. They think that this predisposing developmental deficiency, resting presumably upon some organic peculiarity, limits the infant's capacity to develop and differentiate its ego functions. To this extent meaningful and satisfactory experience with the mother is precluded. In support of this belief is the fact that not all the children of any one "schizophrenogenic" mother are schizophrenic. Some schizophrenics are only children, but most of them do have siblings. These siblings may or may not be psychotic. It must be kept in mind, while developing the concept of the importance of the mother's influence upon the schizophrenic outcome of one of her children, that she often has other children who succumb to no such fate. There is evidently a vast possibility of biological difference in the children of one mother. A peculiar infant understandably exerts an influence upon its mother which may well excite her most unfortunate responses. A normally responsive infant may evoke only her more adequate behavior and so be spared from the problems of dealing with her pathological tensions.

Keeping this consideration in mind, it is, however, also observable that another factor enters into the picture in which one child is normal and another is schizophrenic. Some temporary situations of special difficulty for the mother may have aroused her special morbid needs and drives at the time of the birth and infancy of one child, thereby precipitating her peculiar attitudes in concentrated form upon that child. I think, for instance, of one mother whose schizophrenic child had been conceived while her husband was depressed, and was carried while he was in a

119

mental hospital, where he was expected to die. Another child of this same mother, conceived when father was well and at home, showed no such schizophrenic tendencies. One thinks of another mother who, at the time she was carrying the child who later became schizophrenic, discovered that her husband was unfaithful and, according to her lights, felt that she must divorce him, although this would leave her without support. She thereupon attempted to live with the husband, whom she hated, for the sake of her child. She made it clear to the child that this was a sacrifice which she made for him. There was another mother whose own mother was extremely psychotic and was about to die, so that she felt that she would have no one to help her bring up the baby.

As a result of the very early experiences of these mothers —experiences which have kept them immature and obsessive and hysteric—it is understandable that they have walled themselves in, in order to avoid further insults and damage. In their efforts to achieve healthy and productive living, they actually have been very badly limited, particularly in choice of marital partners. On the basis of much inexperience and prejudice gained from the patients' grandmothers, they have chosen persons as sick and limited as themselves. They have usually chosen persons over whom they assert a superficial dominance, that being the only condition under which they could enter heterosexual relationship. They become disappointed, of course, in such marriages and turn on the children, particularly, in each case, on some one of the children, a great deal of intense emotion which should be shared with another adult and not thrust upon the tender susceptibilities of an infant. The disappointments which these mothers have in reality throw them painfully back into their world of inner objects of love and hate. The child who is being carried at the time of great stress and who comes from within and has recently been a part of the mother is the natural heir to all of her frustrated object-seeking. She invests this child with magically perfect qualities to which she attaches a very intense and demanding love.

Now, for a continuation of such a mystical participation, it is necessary to the mother that the child, however much he may grow, should always remain an infant, utterly dependent and responsive and in need of her love. She can care for him only on these terms. She must not identify him, even in part, with those bad objects of her past experience—the adults, the more successful siblings, and so forth. The more her child comes to resemble older individuals the more he comes under the in-built interdiction of the mother against intimacy with a real and objectively separate person. Particularly, the more he develops his sexual characteristics the more impossible it is for her to accept him. She rejects the boy, the boy's genitality—perhaps through envy and the incestuous threat—and she rejects her daughter through disappointment and fear of rivalry. All this might be expressed by saying that the mother loves excessively, exclusively, and pre-emptively the baby who is her own private fantasy. All through his life he is the one who is expected to live out her unfinished, hopeless aspirations with an outgoing vigor which she does not possess. To the mother this is a matter of her mental life and death. She resists any evidence that the baby is growing up to be just another youngster more like other children than like her dream-baby hero. She not only resists; she does her best to annihilate the evidence, to shame the boy out of his masculinity, the girl out of her femininity—to impress both of them with their undying obligation to her, thanks to the sacrifice she has made.

It follows, of course, that both the boy and the girl are likely to suffer from what Sullivan has called a "primary genital phobia"—that is, an inability to be fully aware of, and accept, their own genitality. For to do so is to bring disaster to the mother. Of course, it is understood that these activities of the mother are carried on preconsciously and that, if they emerge into awareness at all, they are cloaked with suitable rationalizations concerning respectability, hygiene, and so forth. As a general rule these mothers have never mentioned sex frankly and clearly to their children. In so far as these mothers regard their infants as perfect alter egos, they preclude an acceptance of the infants' actual sexual and natural aggressivity. As a result of this, the mother dispossesses the baby of its own bodily and mental integrity. She makes the conditions for its security in living those which meet her own defensive and aggressive requirements to avoid psychosis.

If the foregoing account approximates at all the facts of the life of the mother of the schizophrenic, then it follows that she is really a very anxious, guilt-ridden, ashamed person and that she has lively defenses against her fear, her guilty feeling, and her shame, not to mention her hostility. One defense is anxiety for the child's welfare and his perfection; this anxiety is infectious. The child feels guilty and ashamed rather than confident. Another defense is that of protecting the child from the harsh, crude, adult, sexual persons, so that he comes to share the mother's suspicion and contempt for all those who are different from himself.

I believe that one of the major preoccupations of the schizophrenic patient is the preservation of his ideal mother and her ideals. On the one hand, the patient sees her as domineering, all-powerful, immortal, not in any way to be resisted or opposed. On the other, and with equal intensity, these patients repeatedly—if one is attuned to hear them—report that their mothers are weak, sick, poorly put together, and on the verge of impending mental or physical dissolution. One hears this with increasing frequency once he has learned to expect to hear it. It is not said openly at first but is implied.

One patient, discussing how she would get along with mother on returning home, was asked what she thought of her mother's condition. She answered, "Well, when I brought mother to the hospital—oh, I mean when she brought me to the hospital—she was more nervous than I. She was afraid they would keep her here." Parenthetically, one does not ordinarily ask a schizophrenic patient to make a diagnosis of his mother's condition. There are situations, however, late in treatment in which this is a very pertinent and revealing question. Another patient comes to mind. He came under the care of a young woman physician, who apparently somewhat resembled his mother in appearance. This boy's mother had been a very severe alcoholic. The father had resented and punished the mother by ignoring her. It thereby became the duty of this boy, from the time he was in latency to the mid-teens, to get his mother into the house, upstairs, undressed, cleaned up, and put to bed and fed. He had during these years repeatedly had to undress her, to see her nude, and to take care of her. It was implied that she had made some erotic advances to him. When he was about sixteen, he approached the house one day and saw that there was a commotion. He learned that his mother had, while drunk, killed herself. This patient seemed to like his doctor but, professing great confidence and respect, was never able to tell her anything which might be disturbing to her. Finally it was revealed that he was much concerned about her because in cold weather, when she made rounds and came from another building to his, she would frequently look blue and cold. From this he felt that she was drinking heavily and was about to die. When this patient was ready to leave the hospital, he showed the usual recrudescence of symptoms and reluctance to go and finally acknowledged that the trouble was that, first, he had never told the doctor what he really thought of her. He felt that he ought to do so, but he did not think that she could stand it. Second, he did not think that she could stand his going away and leaving her. This situation was met by the writer's holding a triangular interview with the patient and his doctor so that, being protected by the writer, it was possible for the patient—while looking the other way—to say that there had been times when he had regarded this doctor as a bitch—he thought she drank a great deal too much and was crazy. Having got that out, he glanced sideways and, seeing that the world was still intact, he managed to say that he had come to be very much in love with her and he did not see how she would get along without him. These speeches having been made and the doctor having survived, it became possible eventually for the patient to leave her and the hospital. You will note that this patient said precisely what he meant: namely, that *he* loved her, and he did not think that *she* could get along without him.

These ideas of patients concerning their mothers, fantastic as they may seem, have a basis in reality. There was a schizophrenic patient whose mother stood up bravely, even to the point at which the patient was finally committed to a public hospital where, presumably, she would spend the rest of her days in hopeless dementia. A physician in this hospital undertook intensive and persistent treatment of the patient, and she began to improve. Presently there was some suggestion that plans should be under way for her return to the community. At this point her mother plunged suddenly into a deep, suicidal, psychotic depression. She had to be hospitalized and remained in the hospital for a number of months, silent, unresponsive, defying every suggestion that in any way she might recover. When the subject of her daughter's improvement was taken up, much resentment, confusion, feeling of guilt, and fear came from the patient, with some relief through the catharsis. Eventually she was able to return home, but only on condition that her daughter, when she left the hospital, should not come to live with her.

Even when the schizophrenic patient succeeds in transferring his attachment from his mother to someone who becomes a substitute for her, it frequently happens that this substitute behaves like the mother in that the attachment defies breaking. The substitute is often a homosexual partner, who, if the schizophrenic attempts to desert him, counters with such convincing suicidal threats or physical or mental symptoms as to force the continuance of the relationship. In anticipation of a later chapter, it may be noted here that this pattern is one which the patient will attempt to create in the therapeutic transference situation. He will assume that he is indispensable to the therapist.

One of my patients pointed out that, whenever she got sick, her mother got well; when she got well, her mother got sick. Mother's illnesses were surgical, so it became possible to check on this opinion of the patient, and it was found that it was true. Mother suffered from something which was called "retroperitoneal glands." Whenever the patient was well and at home, mother went to the hospital to have another gland removed and remained comfortably invalided and had a slow convalescence. As soon as the patient began to drink again excessively and have catatonic episodes, the mother improved so that she could take care

126

of her. This had gone on through some five or six different repetitions.

These observations illuminate one meaning of the futility of the dependence-independence struggle of the schizophrenic. It is his belief, based upon his observations, that, if he should improve and become well in the normal sense, his mother would become psychotic. He is aware that, so long as he stays in the hospital and is treated as an infant, mother is somehow secure in that he does not belong to someone else or get really away from her. Were he to become fantastically well, as required in fantasies and expectations, he is aware that he would actually be a paranoid psychotic himself. It seems that these patients prefer to carry the illness, which, as they see it, legitimately emanates from, and, were they to drop it, would return to, their mothers.

There is much more which could be learned about the mothers of schizophrenic patients, and it is good to note that currently a great deal more attention is being paid them than has heretofore been granted. It has been assumed that they were practically inaccessible to treatment—first, because they would not recognize that they were sick, and, second, because they defended themselves against this recognition in order not to suspect that the child's illness had something to do with his experience of them. However, I have known of a few mothers of very sick schizophrenic patients who have, for some reason, submitted themselves to prolonged, intensive psychotherapy. They have in the course of that therapy eventually become able to consider their own psychotic potentialities and, as it were, to lift the burden of carrying these from their children. In these instances patients who otherwise could not have been expected to improve made striking improvement and workable extrahospital adjustments. It does not seem likely that any large numbers of the mothers of schizophrenics will do this.

The fact that a few mothers have done so serves as a pilot experiment, suggesting that it is up to the psychiatrist further to search for ways to make at least some treatment available to the mothers of our patients. In consideration of the great amount of time invested in the intensive treatment of the schizophrenic patient, it would be only good sense to secure that investment by giving some time to his mother. This may have to be done by a different psychiatrist from the one who treats the patient. It may have to be done in the name of treatment of the patient, enlisting the mother's help through regular interviews with her. It is possible that, in that case, it will presently dawn —even on the mother—that the treatment is for herself.

My own limited experience in treating the mother has indicated that the mother—I almost said the "schizophrenogenic mother"—can sometimes transfer her investment in part from her schizophrenic child to the psychiatrist who sees her. This lifts the very heavy burden from the child for a time at least. Of course, if the treatment of the mother is to be effective, it must be sincere. When we regard the mother as a patient, even if she does not know it officially, we do bring to bear upon her whatever benefits accrue from having a therapist, and we do automatically assume a therapist's attitude. These mothers obviously need treatment. Some of them use the opportunity for gaining relief from bottled-up fear, guilt, and resentment. Some may gain some actual insight into their relationship to their schizophrenic child. This is painful and is not to be pushed upon the mother; she must be supported in order to endure it.

Short of actual insight into the two-person involvement, some mothers may be aided to find other interests and investments to replace the schizophrenic child. I know of one seriously discouraged daughter of a composer who was aware of her mother's need that she herself be ill. Then the composer-mother had a composition played by a good orchestra; it was well received. The daughter was present and saw her mother applauded and acclaimed, and then told her psychiatrist, "Now I can get well; mother has her public."

I think that with some change of heart upon the part of psychiatrists, it is quite likely that group therapy for mothers of schizophrenic patients would be time well used both for mothers and for patients. In the group setting, these mothers might be able to tolerate some understanding, to dilute their great sensitivity to criticism.[1]

Before going on from the mothers to another aspect of the background of schizophrenia, something needs to be noted as an apparent exception to the usual family setting

1. Joseph Abrahams and Edith Varon, *Maternal Dependency and Schizophrenia* (New York: International Universities Press, 1953).

which has been presented. Certain schizophrenic patients do not show the usual morbid symbiosis with their mothers; they present a very similar kind of involvement, but it is, rather, with their fathers. This is a phenomenon the meaning of which leaves me without any ready understanding. I therefore merely report the fact and add a few speculative thoughts.

If it is granted that the mother is generally invested by her schizophrenic child with unusually intense meaning and value, it must also be recognized that she herself does not exist as an absolute fact in a vacuum. It has been observed that these mothers are generally married to husbands who are in their way as peculiar as their wives. There is a symbiotic relationship between the two parents, into which the child is introduced and in which the child works out its schizophrenic way of living. Sometimes the child's attitude toward its father appears to be, in fact, the mother's attitude, borrowed or incorporated. In this situation of identification with mother, the child may well be included with her in the father's attitude toward her.

There is one pattern in which the father very early begins to resent his infant son. He resents, apparently, his exclusion from the mother-son intimacy. His expression of his dislike takes the form of contempt for the son's infantile helplessness and for what he sees as the son's effeminacy (identity with mother plus the natural phase in boys of girlish behavior). This contempt can be expressed by grim efforts to "make a man" of the child or by open accusation that he is a sissy or by elaborate neglect.

130

One father, to make a man of his son, subjected him to daily cold shower baths, followed by forcible retraction of his foreskin. Another father laughed at his son's fat little figure and at his poor co-ordination to the extent that the boy came to believe that he could not play baseball, could not even play Ping-pong, and was probably constitutionally homosexual. It was proved that this young man could play tennis, could function heterosexually, and could succeed in masculine competition for money and power. In this instance the mother was the more capable and talented parent. It seemed that the father, unable to overcome his wife in any competition, turned his angry, hurt feeling upon the son, whom he could defeat.

There are also female schizophrenics who are apparently involved more tragically with their fathers than with their mothers. Sometimes these fathers have tried to make men of their daughters; often they have tried to keep the daughters immature and have used them as sexual playthings—have teased, tickled, aroused, and rejected them until they were miserably confused.

There are various circumstances in which it becomes possible for the father to displace the mother in relationship to the child. They include episodes of maternal illness or absence and situations in which the child becomes a pawn in the competitive battle of the parents. They may also include situations which permit the father to be at home a great deal of the time, owing to the nature of his occupation or to his illness. It is easy to see that in these instances father may occasionally abduct the child's dependent investment from the mother to himself.

There is left a problem to which there is as yet no good answer, since there are not available the necessary facts of early history: it is the problem of how the father can participate in the care of the child of less than a year to the extent of displacing the mother in the child's earliest and most compelling expressions of primitive intimacy. The alternative, that the father achieved his influence upon the child much later, seems to mean either that he then displaced the mother, a most difficult feat, or that our theory—that the schizophrenic way of functioning begins before the age of four months—is itself not satisfactory.

This is an area which needs further investigation. There grows out of this problem yet another. Does the presence of the father in the role usually played by the mother change the clinical picture of the patient in any consistent way? I think we may find that, when the father has displaced the mother or has always been the significant figure in the mind of the schizophrenic male, then the patient is more likely to be violent in his defenses against homosexual threats or situations. And perhaps the female schizophrenic whose preoccupations are with her father more than with her mother may prove to exhibit clinically a picture which now is being called "pseudoneurotic schizophrenia resembling hysteria." But these are speculations in need of testing in the course of further therapeutic investigation.

CHAPTER VII

On the Infancy of the Potential
Schizophrenic

Earlier chapters have suggested that acute schizophrenic illness occurs practically always in those whose previous experience and development show considerable deviation from that of normal, merely psychoneurotic, or purely manic-depressive persons. Furthermore, the way of living of those persons who are prone to schizophrenic episodes has been peculiar since infancy. I wish now to suggest a somewhat stronger formulation of the importance of the infantile experience for the schizophrenic way of life. The ability and the necessity to behave schizophrenically or the ability to avoid such schizophrenic behavior is set in all likelihood in infancy. Clearly, this infantile ability or necessity is not absolute, and later specific events may increase or decrease the liability of those who are predisposed to the experience of an actual psychosis. The term "experience" refers to the inner meaning of the events of the life of the schizophrenic and to his reactions to these meanings. Also to be included in this discussion are the absence in the experience of these schizophrenic personalities of certain meaningful relationships and the absence, or the devaluation, of the significance of certain overt happenings which are of considerable importance to most persons.

To proceed with the discussion of the experience of the newborn infant who will later have schizophrenia, let us first consider some of the possibilities of his congenital endowment. Schizophrenic patients are not noticeably unlike other persons at birth or in their very early infancy, at least as they have been observed up to now. I doubt that anyone would feel secure in prophesying from its appearance that a given newborn baby will have process schizophrenia in his later life. However, despite the general similarity of these babies to others, there may be quite important endogenous differences. How much congenital defect there is, is an open question. The present trend in psychiatry is, fortunately, to add to speculation about children—the speculations which have been derived from the treatment of adults—direct observation of infants. This is, of course, a long-term procedure, and it will be some decades before the outcome of current observations will be apparent. In the meantime, in the absence of facts, we may permit ourselves some speculation. We do not know whether character traits, as such, are transmissible. Nor do we know—but we do presume—that the physiological substrate which supports character traits may well be a familial characteristic. That is to say that the predisposition, or the readiness, to become schizophrenic or depressive may be to a degree inborn.

It would seem that the schizophrenic patient is often of the third generation of abnormal persons of whom we can gain some information. The preceding two generations of mothers appear to have been obsessive, schizoid women

134

who did not adjust well to men. There is some evidence that they were, in a sense, immature and that within the obsessive character structure could be found hysterical difficulties. It is to be noted, also, that there are two preceding generations of men who are not masters, or equals, in their own marriages and homes, or psychosexually very successful, and who are often described as immature, alcoholic, and passive, or hard-working, self-centered, and detached from the family. We do not know what sort of mothers and fathers these fathers of schizophrenics may have had, but it could be presumed that the fact that they let themselves be married to mothers of schizophrenics implies something concerning their own mothers.

Loosely, the pattern which emerges is that of two generations of female ancestors who were aggressive, even if in a weak-mannered and tearful way, and two generations of male ancestors who were effeminate, even if the effeminacy was disguised by obsessive or psychopathic tendencies. It might be expected, or at least we would not be surprised to find, that the child of such ancestry would have difficulties centering around the problems of active aggressiveness and passive submissiveness. If the child is unstable in its balance of activity and passivity, the likelihood is that, under the guidance of the sort of mother who gets herself called "schizophrenogenic," the passive behavior will emerge as the overt character of the child, whereas the active behavior will be noted only in the form of negativism, of stubbornness, of retentiveness, and so forth.

Without reference to ancestry, it can be guessed that those children who will be liable to schizophrenia are, upon the whole, victims of a very lively readiness to be anxious—that they will tend to be hypersensitive to danger or to imagined danger. I think that there may well be a constitutional factor in the way in which they react to the danger, real or imagined. Rather than fight, the technique which they employ seems to be that of flight—of quiet, passive withdrawal. They apparently learn early in infancy that one way to quiet down the difficulty and tension existing in the mother-child relationship is to be somnolent, withdrawn, inattentive—apparently asleep. I would suppose that the absence of apparent aggression in response to the manifestations of overt anxiety must mean that the aggression and the anxiety are bound by fantasy rather than by behavior. Furthermore, if there is such a thing as a predisposition to the obsessive character, their histories would indicate that a great many schizophrenic children are so endowed. They are somewhat precocious intellectually, so that they begin to use ego functions for the defenses against anxiety while still in the stage of magical thinking. The result is a strange admixture of logic and magic, that is, the obsessive character overlying infantile anxiety patterns. So much for notions about possible hereditary factors contributing to the situation in which the newborn schizophrenic child finds itself.

Proceeding to the topic of the child's earliest experience of another human being, and assuming that this experience is commonly with the mother, we may repeat some of our observations of her which are most pertinent. Before doing so, it must be said that no one thing in the description of her traits is actually pathognomonic. Every trait which has been ascribed to her is to be found, to some degree, in a good many women who have no schizophrenic children. What is characteristic is no one trait and no one configuration of traits but rather the concentration in one person of an intensity of fixed attitudes and character traits which is unusual. It is the massiveness of the impact of the character of the mother upon her child which impresses it, unrelieved as it appears to be by any adequate compensating attitudes on her part. I believe that the impression which these mothers make upon psychiatrists is an indication of the literal impression which they force upon their infants in their developmental stage. The items in the character of the mother which are of special moment in considering her effect upon her infant are her underlying and pervasive anxiety, some of which would perhaps better be called a "feeling of guilt"; her suspicion of others, of strange people, and so forth; and her avoidance of immediate intimacy. Also, her pattern of denial of unpleasant reality needs emphatic recognition. The result of these attitudes and traits on her part is a person who is emotionally starved and in need of some object to which to attach herself. If she elects to attach herself to the infant, she will use her established technique of control of others by means of tears and suffering, the role of the martyr, the threat of invalidism, and the appearance that she is about to go to pieces.

Probably these habitual character traits of the mother are alone not enough to require that a child be schizophrenic. There is frequently an added factor discernible in a good history in the form of a temporary situational stress during the pregnancy, birth, and infancy of the child. These mothers of schizophrenic children are more introspective and autistic than are the mothers of normal children. In pregnancy it is to be expected that the mother of the schizophrenic entertains excessive conflict about the pregnancy and about the baby. There is evidence that there is a very profound rejection of the reality of the baby as an actual fact and as a person in its own right, and that there is also an exceptional investment in the un-avoidable baby which gives it the quality of an image of great psychological reality to the mother.

The infantile ego contributes to the mother-baby configuration its own main preoccupations, which are self-preservation, security, the reduction of tension and anxiety, so that there may be a comfortable basis for life and growth. Such a baby in interaction with a good mother will, of course, suffer some anxiety, some frustration, but these will be of moderate amount and will be neutralized by mother's support and her own security, so that the child is free to develop and to differentiate. It would seem that the infant whose mother is emotionally ill in the fashion described will itself experience increased anxiety because of increased need and also by empathy or resonance with the mother or by internalizing her. This child, whether or not it has a constitutional liability to anxiety, will be subjected from the beginning recurrently to greater quantities of anxiety than children of good mothers are required to carry. Not only is the child influenced by the mother's anxiety and tensions and difficulties, but the child's evidence of tension and anxiety in response to the mother will, of course, increase the mother's tensions, perhaps to the point at which she no longer is able to function even as a good caretaker of the young animal, the baby. This mutual augmenting of tensions or building-up of reciprocal anxieties would seem to be a factor in disturbing the growth of the infantile ego in such a manner that it becomes liable to schizophrenia. The term "aphanesis," as defined by Ernest Jones, would seem to apply to the state into which these infants must have gone repeatedly. This is a state in which all sensory avenues are open, all stimuli bombard the child uninhibited, and at the same time all avenues of activity and discharge are closed. The child is incapable of any effective behavior, muscular or mental, to relieve the bombardment, the painful stimuli. The device upon which the child would appear to hit is that of going out of contact, becoming somnolent, withdrawn. This, if mistaken by the mother for relaxation and sleep, can permit the child some relief from mother's tensions. It would seem to us that this sort of event, oft-repeated, may be the prototype of the catatonic episodes of later life.

The difficulties of a child in such a situation as this, of course, increase its need of love. By "love" is meant the need of understanding care—care administered by the mother in anticipation of the child's requirements. I would like to insert here a comment that, when we speak of the parental love which the child needs, we are talking about something closely related to what has been discussed elsewhere as "cure" or "psychotherapy" or "treatment" of the patient. However, the difficulties which increase the child's need of love decrease the likelihood that love will be received. If the child remains overtly disturbed, the mother's inefficiency and disability will be increased. If the child becomes quiet, catatonic, the mother will leave it to itself. It must be the case in such a state that the child's natural tendency to feel persecuted is intensified. This tendency must become very intense and a persistent undertone in the attitude of such a child toward the world. Furthermore, a feeling of persecution must require of the child some prematurely contrived defenses, including the withdrawal which has been indicated and various other maneuvers which are found, by trial and error, to diminish the stress existing with the mother.

I feel compelled to digress to comment for the moment upon the animal experiments which demonstrate that animals can be conditioned not to seek food directly but, when they are hungry, to set about certain devious steps which, overcoming various resistances, eventually lead to food. The means to the end—that is, the overcoming of the obstacles and the doing of what might be regarded as irrelevant things—can eventually supersede the end itself and become a new, a pseudo-, end or drive. To be secure, fed, and comforted is an inborn drive, but it can be conditioned so that to please, secure, or quiet the mother becomes what the child experiences as drive. Eventually hunger comes to evoke action to secure the mother's ability to feed the child. In this situation the child might well feel that, in order to nurse the breast, it must first act as a living brassière to support that breast. In order that such a child may satisfy its own need for anaclitic love, it must, first, satisfy its mother's anaclitic requirements!

In terms of the pleasure principle as pronounced by Freud, in which pronouncement pleasure equates with the reduction of tension and the relief or avoidance of anxiety, we may see that for the schizophrenic child the pursuit of the pleasure principle is a very complicated transaction, which involves a train of experiences of the mother known at the beginning merely as a breast, hands, and a voice. This train of experiences is one of uncertainty and discouragement. It contributes to a sense of futility in that the child does not have expectation of regular success in the simple business of being nourished and staying alive. Now, it follows that a breast which is so precariously kept, so easily lost, gets to be overvalued. It would be extremely dangerous for the immature infant to turn any anger overtly upon a mother whose very existence is, in any event, so precarious. At whatever cost, then, to the development of the child, it becomes necessary that the anger be turned elsewhere, that is, be turned inward or contained within the infant. What this containment may do to the development of the homeostatic and other physiologic processes

141

of growth, development, and differentiation, I do not know. I do know that schizophrenic patients have been described, by those who have studied them at length, as physiologically awkward in the same way in which they are psychologically awkward in interpersonal relationships. It has been said of their adrenal function that the only definite way in which it is known to be different from that of other persons is that it is awkward, ill-timed, and therefore inappropriate and somewhat ineffective.[1]

The problem which confronts the newborn infant, part of whose ego is eventually to be relegated to the id, is that there simply is not a sufficiently good mother, nor is the mother sufficiently reliable. The process of living is complicated by the process of supporting the matrix in which to live. I have been saying this in several ways in the preceding paragraphs, partly in the hope that some one of them will impress you and carry the meaning which seems to be in the mind of the schizophrenic, partly because there is no one way of which I am capable which fully expresses the possibilities.

We may suppose that the goodness which a nursing infant takes in from a satisfactory mother is built into the child and becomes its own goodness. This becomes a somatic basis for confidence, satisfaction, and self-esteem, so that eventually the maternal supplies can be relinquished without a feeling of loss, loneliness, and futility. The child

1. Since this was written, Dr. Leopold Bellak has discussed this matter in a paper presented at the annual meeting of the American Psychiatric Association in St. Louis, in May, 1954. He argues convincingly that experiences in the first months may have lasting consequences in patterns of splanchnic behavior.

has, itself, acquired from the mother the substance with which to build the organs by which it can now supply itself. This is true literally, physiologically. I think it is equally factual psychologically. Perhaps the goodness of the mother of the schizophrenic is so conditional, so precarious, that it is never certainly the child's own. The immature ego, or the id, of the schizophrenic child, must therefore fail in some degree to assimilate the good mother into itself. She remains forever an object now present, now gone; when present, now good, now bad. She does not even certainly come to have the value of being something which is owned by the child. The low self-esteem which is conspicuous in all schizophrenic patients may well be a subjective evaluation which the child makes of itself because of this lack of goodness from the mother—lack of built-in, incorporated goodness which it can call its own. The great danger which the child senses in the precarious instability of the mother interdicts anger against her. The child literally believes that anger could destroy the symbiosis and amount, thereby, to suicide. Not only is the anger turned in and made a problem of inner economy both somatic and psychic, but the processes are not established and the techniques are not organized whereby anger and aggression can be directed outward. The child may dream but must not act upon hostile impulse.

It is implied that in the hazardous career of the schizophrenic infant the continuum and cohesion which are essential to a good ego feeling of self and self-sufficiency are frequently disrupted. The development of the ego is irregular. There must follow some clear lack of differentiation, organization, and integration of the various components into a substantial real ego. Much which in a more normal child would go forward with the conscious ego must remain with the infantile ego or id, where it is always a threat to the ego. The threat is that it will emerge in its nonintegrated, unorganized fashion and dominate behavior. This threat is realized in the acute regression to catatonia which must constantly be avoided. All that is remaining in the id, in its attachment everlastingly to the breast, is thereby rendered unavailable to the developing ego. In this sense there is, in the person who has been through these infantile experiences leading to schizophrenia, a relative persistence of large quantities of energy in the form of id. The ego suffers, consequently, and its development and integration are less substantial than those of normal persons. This diminishes the vitality of the sense of self and to that extent diminishes the value which the self puts upon its relation to external objects and its capacity to modify and manipulate them to its own uses. If this were put in psychoanalytic terms, it might be said that the id cathexis to the part object of infancy, the breast, is at the expense of available ego cathexis to real persons and objects in later life. In this sense, to the schizophrenic what we call the "real world" is less real than it is to us, and to him the dream world is considerably more real than it is to us.

If this infantile situation were as altogether desperate as pictured, these children would die. Some of them do. Those who do not must have experienced something of animal comfort in their infancy. Even if they did not get this mothering in their own right as babies, they did get attention and admiration as playthings or as exhibits of their mother's craftsmanship. The little goodness which they do so acquire in the midst of their frustration and fear must be the more overvalued. Many schizophrenic patients do have a sort of narcissism underlying their lack of self-esteem and their futility. This may mean that they feel as if all of the good that there was in the world—the little bit which they got from the breast—is now within them, and everything else is bad. This orientation predisposes to paranoia rather than to healthy development.

When the situation is such that the incentive to active participation by the infant in the emotional life of the actual mother is limited and uncertain, the pattern of preference becomes that for dreamy states, for reminiscences of the good moments, and for avoidance of actual encounters with the real mother. This pattern may begin very early in that it protects the child against eruption of overt anger and retaliation. The evidence that the hostility is deflected is to be found in the frequent histories obtained not from the mother but from some other observer that these to-be-schizophrenic children did have night terrors, fits, and occasional temper tantrums. However, even at the expense of the anxiety of dreams, it would seem that there is a premium which is put upon the id breast dream, the fantasy, at the expense of the value of reality.

Referring once more to Gestalt psychology, an unsolved problem or an incompleted configuration becomes a pseudo-drive; that is, any situation in reality following an unsolved problem, which by association in any way refers to it, tends to be used in an effort to solve the problem or to complete the configuration. It would seem then that the interchange with mother, and later on with others, repeatedly sets off a return to the fantasy of infancy, an effort to solve the problem of the uncertain good-bad breast.

This thought is introduced because it has a definite bearing upon the fate of the schizophrenic patient when he is exposed to classical psychoanalysis. The analyst is —as anyone who has been analyzed knows—of limited and conditional goodness. The neurotic patient can use this situation to bring himself to recognition of the futility of regressive wishes and to their renunciation. The schizophrenic patient, however, can only sense this situation as inviting regressive efforts to re-establish the mouth-breast magical good infancy and to fly forever from any further reality or reality testing. It is because of this striking difference in the orientation of the neurotic and the schizophrenic that psychoanalysts who have endeavored to work with schizophrenics have, in general, abandoned the couch and the invisibility of the analyst and have preferred to work with these patients face to face, keeping the reality always in evidence. They have also preferred to deal with current problems and the techniques the patient is currently using in his relationships to others rather than to encourage fantasy and dream. This will explain also why the psychoanalyst working with schizophrenics tends more to endeavor to clarify his relationship with the patient as it now is and less to try to relate it to the early infantile situations so that it will be grasped as a transference. The truth is that the schizophrenic does not grasp it as a transference but sees it as a reality. In this same frame of reference it becomes clear why many psychoanalysts do not in any way endeavor to interpret the positive transference of schizophrenic patients or to interpret any good internalizing and identifying the patient may do with the analyst. It becomes equally clear why they are always quick to bring to the patient's awareness his hostility toward them, not merely as transference but as a fact— something which they now feel toward the analyst. This is done, in large part, in order that the schizophrenic may learn that it is safe to feel angry toward one upon whom you are dependent.

One would suppose that the potentially schizophrenic infant would try to escape from his difficulties with his mother by early and repeated transferences of the problem to his relations with other persons, such as father and older sibling. It appears that he does attempt this maneuver. It may often succeed, and then by amelioration of the painful fixation it may come about that the infant very largely escapes his liability to schizophrenia. In that case we do not find him in this series of patients, although, were he to come to analysis for psychoneurotic difficulties, his analytic material might show schizophrenic techniques in his more archaic associations.

Frequently the maneuver is not successful, and the

infant does not escape into intimate growing experiences with persons other than the mother. One reason for his failure is that the most probable substitute for mother, in the actual situation, is the maternal grandmother or an older sister or both. These ladies are quite prone to operate within the same general orientation to life which affects and afflicts the mother herself. Another interlocking reason for failure to escape is that one of the mother's most stringent regulations imposed upon the child is that he shall have no other mothers or gods before her. She permits relations only with those who cannot displace her.

In reference to the mother's interdiction of intimacy with, and response to, others than herself, we have moved on from considering the id experience of earliest infancy and have come to a discussion of the stage of development of the superego. In this phase of experience part of the child's ego devotes itself to an integration with the presence of the mother within the ego. This is the presence of one who approves or disapproves, loves or withholds love. It must be determined by the infant, if possible, what behavior she likes and what she dislikes and also what rewards and punishments she dispenses.

The mother of the schizophrenic will contribute to her child's superego, as would any other mother, that version of the mores with which her own superego is enlightened, somewhat modified, probably, by her more recent experiences and more conscious ego ideals. In the case of the mother of the schizophrenic, from our observations of her character we can anticipate part of what this contribution will be. Her obsessional attitudes will indoctrinate her child with rigid ideas of the virtues of cleanliness, orderliness, parsimony, and reaction formation against hostility. All these virtues will tend to interdict spontaneity, intimacy, and generosity or tolerance. Occasionally the obsessive mother, rather than superimpose herself upon the child, will transmit a countercompulsive set of rules which deny the child responsibilities or independence and require of him that he be a spoiled baby or a privileged genius in the making. The result is a superego which rewards carelessness, disorderliness, unproductivity, and spendthrift ways as evidence of artistic temperament and great promise for the future. The practical effect, of course, is to compel the child to remain helplessly dependent upon the mother, who can then be justified in taking care of him. In terms of physical behavior, an example of this pattern is that of an obsessive mother, constantly preoccupied with cleanliness and fear of dirt, whose child persists in having diarrhea so that the mother continually has to clean him. When the mother gains some understanding and modification of her attitudes, the child does not need to have diarrhea. These acquisitions from the mother are not of the essence of the schizophrenic quality of the superego which we are discussing. They are found frequently in psychoneurotics and neurotic characters, in infantile personalities, and, as in the example immediately given, in psychosomatic disorders.

That which appears nearly specific for schizophrenia is the means of disapproval and punishment which the superego uses to threaten the child. It must be remembered that this superego, as it emerges, is quite similar to the behavior of the mother. The threat is that the mother will suffer, will collapse and die, leaving the child helpless and alone. This is no idle threat. The child has frequently seen her disintegrate to the point where she was not in good contact and was not able to give efficient care and to the point that her emotions overflowed and flooded the child. Those of us who have actually accepted the teachings of our parents and have incorporated them into our own ethical ideals and behavior have thereby acquired self-confidence and the ability to share experience with others. We can afford to dissolve our dependence upon the superego for companionship and protection. It is therefore difficult for us to understand why anyone would go through life according to a set of rules which did not further his ego designs for self-realization and did not make good sense to him. But the schizophrenic does not have any belief in the possibility of self-realization, except in terms of sacrifice to preserve the mother. He does not have confidence in his ability to relate satisfactorily to anyone other than the mother. It becomes clear, when this quality of the superego of the schizophrenic is realized by the therapist, that he cannot rely upon the motivation of the patient to aid in any recovery which implies separation from, and damage to, the presence of the mother. It is as if she, in the role of superego, must live and be obeyed; otherwise she, as the object of the infantile ego or id, as the nourishing breast, is forever lost. What is a schizophrenic profited if he shall gain the whole world and lose his own mother? When we enter into diplomatic relations with the schizophrenic patient for therapeutic purposes, we encounter this basic morality of his. We find that it supersedes in its insistence all the other ideals commonly found in patients. It would not be putting it too sharply if we said that, for the schizophrenic to gain that independence from his infantile superego which is one of the goals of psychoanalysis is in his feelings fully equivalent to his murder of his mother. That is horrible enough even in our perspective; it is much worse in his because it destroys all purpose and all supplies for further living.

We come now to comment upon a characteristic of schizophrenic behavior which is indeed baffling. It is that the patient who remains so bound to the presence of his mother is not thereby, by any means, blinded to her observable characteristics. All the relevant facts of the situation in relation to her were known to the patient even as a child, but these facts cannot be faced and surmounted. They cannot be overcome by resort to any strategy of a higher integration, nor can they be very much modified by the acquisitions of further experiences of the mother or of other women. Most of the lives of these patients after infancy are mere repetitions, with variations, upon a limited number of early patterns of relationship to the mother. It is not safe, and there is not sufficient incentive for new adventures in intimacy. The summation of the futility of this situation is crippling.

Although the facts are known about the mother, there is failure to evaluate the actual mother in any practical frame of reference. At most, the schizophrenic patient refuses to see her from time to time, or, when seeing her, he may become disturbed. Efforts to induce such patients to make practical decisions based upon the facts meet intense opposition which will go so far as to plunge them back into acute confusional psychosis. The known fact of the limited goodness for the patient of the actual mother and of her nearly unlimited badness for him rarely becomes the basis for appropriate renunciation by the patient and separation from her.

In considering the infancy of the schizophrenia-prone child and that of the schizophrenia-proof child, four postulates have been made. The first of these is that the infant-mouth, mother-breast configuration, which we call the "id," is so distorted by vastly greater mutual anxiety in the case of the schizophrenic infant that it suffers thereafter a pathologic relationship to the ego of the child. The desperate devices resorted to by the infant to survive and to defend its ego result in a withdrawal from the id whereby large amounts of energy remain in the id, unavailable to the ego. The consequent ego defect interferes with the working-out of sublimated satisfactions. The excess of id is held under precarious repression and dissociation. It threatens to erupt in any specifically appropriate situation and to evidence itself in ego dystonic and disruptive archaic activity.

The second postulate is that the configuration which we

call "ego-superego," specifically, the infantile ego in relation to the powerful, depriving, and punishing mother-presence, contains within the schizophrenic psyche an amount of destructiveness which is a very great threat to the integrity of the ego. I wish to emphasize here that the expression of anger and the release of tension through aggressive activity, which constitute the behavior of a normal infant, are very largely interdicted in the schizophrenic. This does not destroy his anger, and it is hard to overestimate the amount of hostility which is, in its immature form, latent within him. Also, it is apparent that to the infant the mother herself is possessed of an equally angry and hateful destructiveness. If this were not so, he would not effectively renounce his own expression thereof. It follows, then, that in addition to great anger there is fear. The combination amounts to lasting hate of which the patient is profoundly unaware. At least he feels unable to do anything overt about it. There are, therefore, repeated sabotage and denial of ego intentions; and there is danger constantly of invasion of primitive superego demands which will disorganize the ego into a psychosis. It is probable that this intensely powerful superego, kept precariously out of the ego by heavily guarded boundaries, acts itself as a further repressing force against the id, so that the id impulses are doubly repressed, lying beneath ego and superego.

A third postulate is that an ego which emerges from such an infancy as this is inadequate to the requirements of healthy living. Only in limited areas can it function safely. These areas may be large if they do not conflict with the superego, that is, with the mother's ideas as understood by the child. Much may be accomplished if it is in imitation of someone approved by the mother or in some way not a serious step away from the mother. But the life of the schizophrenic between infancy and adolescence and thereafter is peculiarly devoid of events which ripen and deepen, develop, and differentiate the ego functions of living intimately with its compeers. Psychosexual development, in particular, is scanty and shallow, and therefore a great motive for struggle to succeed in the world is depreciated and lost. "Money, power, and the love of women" are not the goals of the schizophrenic.

One last postulate is that, when the ego does come to grief and disaster, it is as the result of a situation of temptation to a desired relationship with someone. This specifically mobilizes threats from the superego and impulses from the id to such infantile activity as to re-create a panic patterned closely after the anxiety attacks of infancy. In this sense infantile experiences do set the stage for very precisely disastrous repetitions in later life. I mention the precision and specificity of the tempting situation and the triggering mechanism because it is observable that schizophrenics who break badly in specific situations are much less vulnerable than neurotic or even normal persons to a great many nonspecific assaults.

This point can be illustrated by an account of two schizophrenic patients who precipitated in each other acute episodes predetermined by their relationships in youth to their mothers. This is the story: The young man, who had been acutely ill and was improving, was courting a young woman whom he knew to have had previous heterosexual experiences. In her presence he had an erection, which he made so little effort to conceal that it was visible through his clothing. When it was certain that she had seen it, he proceeded to give her a moral speech, telling her how delightful it would be if they could cohabit. This, he said, he could not consider because of her purity, her goodness, her nobility, and the fineness of her femininity; she was so like his mother that he could not think of degrading her. The young lady, knowing that he knew she was not averse to or inexperienced in extramarital intercourse, was furious. She counterattacked in his most vulnerable spot. She knew that he had been preoccupied, while acutely ill, with homosexual fears and had only recently had self-confidence enough to enjoy dancing with a few women patients. So she went to them and told them he was a homosexual and an exhibitionist. They taunted him with this, and he promptly withdrew into a confused and semistuporous psychosis lasting some weeks. On learning of this eventual outcome of her talk, the young lady became agitated and then apathetic. She was ill for several weeks. Knowing a little more about both these patients and their history than is here recounted, it seems very clear that each was visiting an appropriate punishment upon the surrogate for a seducing, rejecting, and punishing parent. The point of the story is that they managed to ventilate and exercise a little vindictiveness at a terrific cost to themselves.

Nearly everyone has some sort of conscience, and, if he studies it, he will find in it a good bit which surpasses any customary ethical standards in its severities and its primitive cruelty. The schizophrenic differs from the rest of us in that his superego is to him a very real person within him, who not only advises and threatens or opposes but actually dominates his life with crippling restrictions and interdictions supported by the threat that the superego itself will go crazy. You and I can, on occasion, defy our conscience and feel the better for it. The schizophrenic, when he breaks with his, loses all hope of ever finding any security, any physiological comfort, let alone erotic satisfaction. He loses every possibility in the world. Knowing this, he gives up in advance to his superego and avoids any real experience of intimacy which might be tempting and which might also be educational. When he does break through—and he does from time to time—the fear and guilt are such that he is completely at the mercy of the superego and of the id. He then is unable to exercise the functions of perception, thought, and controlled action. Panic takes over.

The foregoing chapters present the writer's present understanding of the nature of the schizophrenic situation and attitude toward life. From such an understanding there comes recognition that schizophrenic patients can be expected to relate to therapists only within limitations which are the essence of their difficulty in living. For them the therapeutic situation is inevitably a dangerous one. But, if the therapist respects the danger signs, the schizophrenic patient may be able to work with him to great advantage. Further discussion of therapeutic intervention in schizophrenia concerns itself with the interaction upon each other of therapist and patient.

CHAPTER VIII

Psychotherapy—the Patient's Contribution

Psychotherapeutic intervention in schizophrenia is a special instance of psychotherapy in general. It is grounded in those principles which have emerged from psychoanalytic research. To be kept in mind are such concepts as these: The patient defends himself in a variety of ways, some of which close his mind against awareness of what is going on. These defenses are put into action whenever anxiety threatens. Patients in need of psychotherapy are relatively intolerant of anxiety. They tend to avoid it so effectively that they are unable or unwilling to know what it is actually about. They do not, therefore, tend to test the reality of their environment or of their inner experience. It is a primary purpose of psychoanalytic therapy to aid the patient to tolerate anxiety sufficiently to dispense with defensive repressions, amnesias, inhibitions, denials, regressions, displacements, distortions, and so on, so that he may know what he feels and thinks and what drives impel him. In order to do this, the patient's interest in himself and his sense of his own worth must be supported by the therapist.

If the patient is to be able to use his therapist and the therapeutic situation to the end that his ego functions improve in their effectiveness to bring about security and the ability to achieve satisfaction in the processes of living in the real world of human relatedness, he must come into treatment with some resources. Among these resources are at least some fragments of ego functioning by means of which he can perceive that someone in the environment is doing something in relation to him. For example, there was a psychotic woman, one of whose delusions was that she was a young man who was in love with and going to marry a girl whose name was hers and whose appearance was her own. Failing in the accomplishment of this fantasy, she became mute, retarded, and unresponsive to anyone. She had been in this state for some months when I undertook to treat her. She was brought, without her co-operation, to my office daily, seven days a week. I spent at least half an hour daily speaking to her, remarking upon her condition in terms of evidence of her pain and discomfort and some ideas I had about why she was feeling so miserable. At the beginning of treatment she was mute and sullen, averted her face, and appeared not to hear me; but the nurses reported that her sleep improved, that she ate with less persuasion, and, after a time, that she became less retarded and indifferent when they dressed her to come to my office. She began to try to comb her own hair, to put her stockings on with care that the seams were straight, and to select the dress she would wear. She occasionally spoke, slowly and uncertainly, in short sentences, all expressing discouragement and sadness. Finally, after about six months, during which her general behavior had improved, she looked up at me one day and asked, with emphatic dis-

159

taste and anger, "Who in hell buys your neckties?" It was the beginning of over two years of verbal participation on her part in therapy. She stated that the neckties meant to her that I was married and not available to her. She was very angry that I had attracted to myself her desires. Only after a year of further treatment did she see any relationship between her involvement with me, a married man twice her age, and the fact that her father had been quite seductive and then had deserted her. This realization came about in a fortuitous circumstance. One day I had come directly from a barber-shop to the hour with her. The barber had applied a good quantity of hair tonic to my head, something I ordinarily did not permit him to do. The patient became agitated and frightened. She said she must be hallucinating again—she felt that her father was in the room. Our talk about this feeling of his presence brought out the explanation that she smelled him, something that he used on his hair. She was relieved to find that she actually smelled the tonic and that she was not hallucinating. I was relieved that a way was found for discussing her feelings about me in terms of the history of her previous, and for some years buried, feelings about her father. It explained the meaning of much of her behavior and much of her interpretation of my activity in relation to her. This working-out of a part of her transference tended to free appreciable amounts of her interest to be invested in other men not so similar to her father, and this interest contributed an incentive to get herself out of the hospital so that she could participate in social situations appropriate to her age.

In telling this story, note is made of another ego resource necessary for the undertaking of psychotherapy. It is a motive for recovery, for the return to reality, and for the discovery of new reality. The desire of this young woman to get herself well enough to live in a setting in which she could go to parties, dance and date, and find a partner in love came to light late in treatment, but the desire to have some relationship with someone, to escape from the solitude of psychotic regression, had appeared very early in treatment in the form of efforts to make herself presentable and attractive. To look even further back for a motive on her part to relate to me, it can be reported that I, who had seen this patient in an earlier phase of her illness, had felt an interest in her. Part of this was, in truth, a transference on my part. She reminded me of a younger sister. This resemblance could be rationalized as a similarity of complexion and body build, but that would be a reduction to concrete terms of something which had more potency. The something was that this patient, although acutely disturbed, still conveyed to me some impression of a healthy little girl, a vivacious child who was hidden beneath the incrustations of a dozen years of devastating, tragic mental illness.

This last observation calls attention to another ego resource requisite for the patient who would make use of therapy. It is the ability to communicate something significant to another person and to receive, even in a distorted form, after much resistance, some answer to the communication. It was learned from the patient referred to above in our later work that, when I first saw her, she was feeling utterly deserted. Those who were in charge of her appeared to her to be perfunctory, obtuse, and even cruelly resentful. She remembered our first very brief meeting when she was nude in the seclusion room. At that time she had felt that here was someone who at least felt no ill-will and at last saw the human being so befogged in madness. She wanted to talk to me but could not at that time. Before leaving the discussion of this patient, it should be clarified that she was suffering from a schizo-affective disorder. The retardation and sadness referred to were part of her depressive condition and not of her schizophrenia.

Some bit of functioning perceptive ego and some ability to communicate are among the requirements for participation in therapy, but they are not of themselves sufficient. There are others, such as a little talent for recognition of what goes on in your mind and behavior and a not-too-great satisfaction in the secondary gains from the illness. The one outstanding requirement, if psychotherapy is to go beyond the modification of a few symptoms and is to accomplish any lasting and significant reorganization of the patient's character, is that the patient be able to concentrate his diffuse neurosis or psychosis into a transference neurosis or psychosis, in which the difficulties of a lifetime are focused, and currently felt to exist, in the patient-therapist configuration. Without this emergence of the transference-resistance situation, therapy remains impersonal, somewhat sterile, and academic. With the transference psychosis established, there exists a present, vital, personal conflict which potentially is soluble by means of mutual working-through.

In the preceding chapters I have presented some observations and some formulations derived from them for the purpose of understanding the peculiarity of schizophrenia as a pattern of human behavior from infancy on through psychotic episodes in adult life. These observations and assumptions, if correct, should offer some forecast concerning the schizophrenic performance in the psychotherapeutic situation. If it is assumed for the present that the psychotherapist is competent and reliable and is, so to speak, a fixed quantity, then the assumption can be made that the schizophrenic will differ from other patients in some predictable ways. Of course, each schizophrenic patient has his own identifying personal qualities in which he varies from any other schizophrenic, but it is still worth while to consider how schizophrenic patients, as a group, do resemble one another and how they differ from other groups of persons in their approach to psychotherapy.

The functional integrity of a working amount of ego which is requisite for a formal and classical psychoanalysis is not to be expected in any but the mildest of schizophrenic afflictions, and then not until considerable gains have been established through preparatory treatment. Here the expression "mildest of schizophrenic afflictions" needs scrutiny. Mildness of involvement is not to be confused with absence of dramatic symptom formation. There exist persons who get along quietly, do their work adequately, and appear only mildly distressed, yet are unable to distinguish between daydreams and waking reality, who have no objectively valid relationships of any depth with other persons, and who can function adequately only in the narrow, monotonous, unchanging, simple situations to which they have become accustomed. Many of these persons have had an acute schizophrenic illness some years ago. For example, a single woman of forty-four, a physical therapist, who lived alone with her maiden aunt, age sixty-five, had been getting along with her job for over twenty years. She was used to going to church with her aunt, going on vacations to the beach with her, and playing cards once a week with three other single women. She went to the movies twice a week alone. Her aunt had been becoming short of breath recently and also short of temper and of memory. The doctor told this patient that her aunt was ill and probably would not live very long. The patient thereupon began to resent and quarrel with the aunt. She wanted to go out more frequently than the aunt could manage; she did not want to take care of the old lady or of the apartment. She wanted to buy her own clothes unaided by this aunt, something she had never done. She became sleepless, restless, and, in a word, anxious. The doctor gave her bromides and hormones. Her anxiety increased. She entertained some rudimentary plans to go on a vacation alone. This, the aunt thought, was going too far, so she arranged to get the patient to a psychiatrist. It must be reported that this psychiatrist was not the standard, reliable, competent one to whom we have referred. He was, moreover, curious about psychoanalysis, so he put the patient on a couch four times a week and listened to her while he encouraged the "free association" which rapidly began to sound, even to him, like delusions and schizophrenic fantasies. The patient felt desperate, unable to work, and as if she was literally going to pieces mentally. The psychiatrist also felt uneasy to the point of alarm. He called for a consultation. Now it is a tradition of the profession that we take care of one another, so the consultant was doubly motivated to protect his colleague and to take over the care of this patient. Perhaps her hospitalization could be prevented. Therefore, he undertook her treatment, requiring that she sit up and face him. He held her attention by guiding questions about her and her life. He refused to prescribe further medication of any sort for her but rather firmly insisted on "working out" with her what she was to eat, since she had been losing weight; when she should go to bed—she had been staying up part of the night; what part of the work she should do in the apartment; and what plans she could devise for her impending vacation. During this process of supporting her ego and directing it to resume its usual responsibilities, he heard from her that when she was about twenty she had gone to college to become a student of English. In her first year, however, she fell in love with a classmate, a girl. This girl introduced her to some heavy "spooning." This word will date this patient for older readers. The patient felt guilty, ashamed, angry, and fascinated. At the height of her conflict her partner suddenly and contemptuously jilted her. Her story then became confused. She thinks that within a few days her mother took her home, where she was in bed, was spoon-fed by the mother, and was untidy. She was ill for about six months. Thanks to the mother's nursing, she recovered and returned to college, but now she took a less taxing course, that is, one in physical education rather than in English. She got a job and held it until her mother died; her aunt took her in, and she got a similar job, which she still was holding. She had occasionally wondered about her aunt's health—what to do if she died. There were vague preoccupations, particularly with the problem of doing something about the corpse. Would she have to have it buried? Beneath this was the question of what she would do with herself: With whom would she live? Or would she perhaps also die? At this point in the recounting of her terror at the loss of her mother, and now at that of her aunt, the patient suddenly changed her manner, asked for a cigarette (she did not ordinarily smoke), spoke of having a cocktail (she never had drunk), and, with a peal of empty laughter, demanded to know "when we girls [self and aunt] will be old enough to have dates with boys." She proceeded to declare her love for the first psychiatrist she had seen and her grief that he had rejected her. She wanted to know then whether doctors ever kissed patients. Asked why she brought this up, she said that she thought they sometimes did. Once she was constipated and went to a chiropractor, who washed out her colon, rubbed her back, kissed her, and charged her three dollars. At this point she looked quite coquettishly at the therapist who brought her back from this flight to further talk about her aunt's health—what would in fact be necessary when she died. Plans were made and eventually carried out for the patient to get her aunt into the care of a relative who grasped something of the situation and then to get herself into living quarters with three other maiden ladies whom she knew. Her social activities, such as they were, were resumed. She decided that she would rather save her money for a vacation than continue treatment, particularly since the analyst did not include kissing as part of his technique. This patient had a small inheritance, and she would be entitled to a pension in a few years. Her old age then would be moderately secure financially. Meantime, she would enjoy playing cards with her girl friends, going to the movies, attending to her work, and, adventure of adventures, going on a vacation without her aunt. And, if she needed it, she added that she might go to the chiropractor now and then for another treatment.

This patient was what is sometimes called a "burned-out" schizophrenic. Her acute illness was so treated by her mother that, although she recovered from it, she never again had any mature experience with another human being. But she was not entirely burned out. The id is persistent. Under the provocation of great need for dependency and the fear of being deserted, and with an encouraging psychiatrist, her interests flared up once more into adolescent fervor, in which they had been interrupted in her original illness. The emptiness of her life since then did not mean that she could use psychoanalytic therapy. It rather indicated the necessity of restoring to her such limited function as she had and of re-establishing such defenses as she was accustomed to depend upon.

Another patient demonstrated that, even when hallucinating and deluded, excited and requiring emergency hospitalization, he still possessed sufficient organized ego ability to get into and to use psychoanalytically oriented therapy, couch and all. This young man was the son of a paranoid woman who had told him that it was a good thing his father had died when the patient was only four: it removed a bad influence from his life. The patient had a sister who in appearance and professional interest much resembled the therapist with whom this patient came to work. The patient was his mother's special creation. He sang and he played the piano to her delight. He was an honor student and graduated into a prized job with a famous company of engineers. Men were often attracted to him and occasionally made sexual advances. There were one or two occasions in his early youth when he submitted to fellatio. Women were attracted to him. An uncommon number of these, he later learned, were Lesbian, or at least he thought they were. He liked their society. He fell in love once, when he was seven years old. The little girl wore a brown silk dress and had brown eyes. Telling about her during a treatment hour, the patient suddenly reported with a start that she was now sitting on a little shelf on the wall looking at him. There was actually no shelf. During his professional career this young man went out with his colleagues and, because he did not want them to think him queer, occasionally had intercourse with a party girl.

After a few years, the firm for which he worked decided to raise two of its employees to junior partnership. The patient was perhaps the brightest of the five candidates, but he was not chosen. He complained about this and was told that he did not have the personality for executive work. He could stay on as a worker doing technical detail. In the next few months he became aware that strange things went on in the office. One day six men came out of the boss's office carrying a coffin. The patient looked into it and saw the boss smoking a cigar. Several men, including those who had been promoted, began to sneer at him and to call him "queer." They drank together, and he saw one of them kiss another on the stairway in broad daylight. The coffin appeared again and again. The patient appealed to his sister, who recognized his condition. In his anxious tension and near-panic he made some effort to embrace her. She was not certain whether he was trying to seduce her or to kill her. On the way to the hospital the patient spent a night with his uncle, sleeping in the same bed with him. He slept very deeply, as if drugged. In the morning he saw a spot of blood on the outside of the seat of his pajamas. It meant to him that his uncle had had anal relations with him. In great agitation he hastened to the hospital. In response to the psychiatrist's efforts to get his history and to determine his mental status, he was flippant, sarcastic, facetious, angry, and finally coldly, politely unwilling to talk further with him. It may be remarked that this psychiatrist was a reserved, obsessive, correct young man, who at the time of this interview was in a phase of development in which he was directive and restrictive with his patients, particularly discouraging their sexual interests. Later that day the patient saw another psychiatrist, to whom he told the story which has been outlined. After mentioning the blood-stained pajamas, he grew very serious and confided that he knew what was the matter with him. It was absolutely true that if he had married a girl like his sister, he would never have got so mixed up. Something in the impact of this statement itself, or something in the psychiatrist's reaction, was too much for the patient's self-restraint. He leaped into the air, screamed, hid himself behind a large chair, and cried out, "Now I have told you too much. You know too much. I want you to go." The psychiatrist went, and to this day he wonders if it was not a mistake. There must have been a great deal in this patient that required that he not be left alone. As it was, he was transferred to a disturbed service, where he remained nearly five months. The psychiatrist tried to resume their talk on the day after this episode, but the patient would have nothing to do with him and acted, in fact, as if he did not know him. During the five months of disturbance this patient did his convincing best to be manic. He was vividly overactive, slept little, talked a great deal, was contemptuous, and continually tormented both patients and nurses. He liked to trip older men. He liked to lift up the nurses' skirts. When approached by any psychiatrist, he became abusive, threatening, paranoid in his accusations, and, if it was necessary to end the interview, quite incoherent, gesturing and spitting. When he wore out this defensive role and regained an open service in the hospital, he came one day to the office of the psychiatrist to whom he had confided. He banged on the door. Without waiting for an answer, he thrust it open, stalked in, and placed himself upon the analytic couch. He returned regularly, daily, even for over a year after he was discharged from the hospital. To the accompaniment, or incidental music, of much angry accusation, changing quickly to silly love-making talk and often to archaic symbolic utterances about sun-worship, the sex of the sun, and the effect of it on his inner states, he managed to carry on a meaningful investigation of himself and his character, of the reasons why it was unavoidable that he "go crazy," of the situation in which he now found himself, of the steps he planned to take to re-establish himself in a new plan to work. There emerged great depth of feeling for a little boy whom he had found and who stood for himself. He wished to be the therapist's little boy, so he did for this new-found waif what he wanted done for himself. His attitude toward his therapist ranged from anguished appeal when he got into trouble, which he did several times, to a rather girlish, coquettish intimacy and to occasional expressions of respect. This patient carefully avoided any sexual acts with his unofficially adopted little boy. He did get into some homosexual encounters for a while with strangers who invariably robbed, beat, and humiliated him. This was not fully worked out, but he managed to see a self-destructiveness in these acts and to contain it. For over a decade he has lived within the requirements of his professional environment and the community and has appeared to be content with himself. He never communicates with his therapist.

This account is given because it shows that, for all the gravity of his acute illness, he was able to discover the possibility of intensive therapy and to select his therapist. However unusual and impulsive his presentation of himself for treatment, his discernment was such that he got himself to one who could work with him; that he did not make more progress in his treatment was not altogether his fault. There was available only one other therapist more skilled than the one he chose, and that one was discouraged from any interest in working with him by the fact of his manic-like episode. The patient knew somehow that this therapist did not like him, so he bowed to necessity and selected the less competent one.

This patient illustrates a situation which is very frequently encountered. It is one in which it appears that the ego is in sad disorder, being unable to cope with hallucinations, delusions, and impulses. Sometimes the apparent disruption permits misidentifications, disorientation, confusion, and incoherence. Yet, in the midst of all the evidence of functional decompensation, it can be seen that the patient is, in a sense, well aware of his orientation and of the identity of himself and of others; is capable of coherent, relevant observation; and knows that his delusions are not really true and that his hallucinations are not actual external phenomena. It may well be that the patient experiences two sets of phenomena simultaneously and, to protect himself from confusion, elects to accent, believe in, and feel the validity of one to the neglect and disavowal of the other. It is sometimes observed that he may, under pressure of changed sources of anxiety, quickly move his validating recognition from the one set of experiences to the other. This all adds up to the fact that it is not easy to assess with any accuracy the present or potential available assets of the ego of the schizophrenic patient. More errors are certainly made in the direction of assuming that schizophrenics are deteriorated, dilapidated, completely lost in fantasy, and out of all useful contact, so that they are unavailable for psychotherapy, than in the contrary direction of expecting of them more than they are potentially able to perform, given proper security and motivation.

Some schizophrenic patients stoutly assert that they could conduct themselves in a normal manner if they wanted to, that is, if they were permitted to leave the hospital. They say that their regressive acts are deliberate or careless or vengeful, when the evidence is that, in fact, they cannot manage themselves and are whistling in the dark to calm their fears of further disruption. Many schizophrenics do conceal from the observer the fact that they are preoccupied with hallucinations, delusions, compulsive ideas, and ritualistic defenses, but, before deciding that a schizophrenic patient is out of contact or is snowed under by id impulses and superego criticisms to the extent of being inaccessible, it is a good thing to consider what may be his motives for withdrawal from the world, or from you, and what factors may contribute to his lack of enthusiasm for our so highly prized reality.

Whether or not the will to recover is inherent in all persons probably is dependent upon the definition of recovery. That not all the regression and disruption of the thinking process in schizophrenics is an inevitable defect is demonstrated by those patients who become incoherent when a too painful idea presents and again become coherent when it is pointed out to them that they are defending themselves in this way. It will be noted that at times these patients do seem to be unable to recognize their defensive regression until it is described to them by an acceptable therapist. There is much reason to believe that the motivation to recover, as commonly understood, is very weak in most schizophrenics. They would certainly desire relief from anxiety and from futile loneliness. Some would agree that a fantasy world is empty and purposeless, and they would give lip service, at least, to the superiority of a full and purposeful life. But very many schizophrenics are definite in their assertions that, as they see it, healthy or normal persons are dead, unimaginative. They are slaves of conventional, competitive strivings for a worthless material and social prominence. One thinks that these comments refer perhaps to the ambitious parents. Some basis for this attitude, of course, is sensed by a good many persons who are not even remotely schizophrenic. But one can think that there is also an element of sour grapes in a schizophrenic's rejection of normal aspirations as not worth the effort, for the truth is that he does not think that he could succeed even if he made the effort.

The schizophrenic's preference for words rather than for acts and his investment of words with the magical value of acts accomplished lead him to say that he is going to be a great champion or genius, and to leave it there, without further efforts or plans. Has he not said it? Very many of these patients do not say that they are mentally ill. They say that they are well and blame their difficulties upon persecution, influences, and misunderstandings. This position is a sort of short circuit preventing recognition of the dreadful fact of the psychosis and also thereby precluding any serious efforts toward recovery. Whatever steps are taken by these patients are for the purpose of stopping the persecution, neutralizing the influences, or convincing the doctor by repetitive statements that they are well.

There are at least two further factors which diminish or negate the will to recovery in these patients. One of these is that the patient has never been free and spontaneous, never available for objective intimacy with others. He has, therefore, no memories of normality and cannot grasp its implications. It is a new experience and as such is feared and devalued. The other reason for not striving for actual recovery is also the reason that accounts for the absence of new experience, of adventure, and of mature sharing of experience. It is and has been true of the patient that the presence of his mother, or, occasionally, of his father, has interdicted all new experience, all spontaneous self-directed relationship to reality. Put otherwise, the possessive and destructive superego will tolerate no rivals and no escape from the preplanned servitude to it.

And yet, with these powerful motivations to stay away from ordinary normality, schizophrenic patients do experience an urge to seek understanding and at least to identify themselves with the therapist. By way of much subtle testing they do make some efforts to establish constructive rapport with him. The source of this drive perhaps can be traced all the way back to the early infant-mother, mouth-breast configuration—that is, to the drive of the id toward a satisfaction in relation to objects.

This brings up the problem of communication without which psychotherapy becomes a game of hide and seek. It may be said at once that schizophrenics present in this area their familiar ambivalence. They wish to be understood, but they fear to be. They usually have had much experience during and after earliest childhood playing verbal hide and seek with mother or father. In these games they speak in riddles, expressing themselves by opposites, making diplomatic announcements which may mean what they say or more probably mean only to allay the listener's undue curiosity or anxiety or tendency to interfere. There is a good bit of testing in this process. If you know what the patient means, then he need not say it. If you do not know, then you are not attuned to him, and you prefer to believe something other than fact. So he tests his therapist with statements made to find out what the latter is most willing to believe. Does he actually want to know the patient's thoughts as they are? Or does he prefer to be told that the patient's thoughts are those which he wishes them to be? Verbal communications are often so blunt that they say or ask two contradictory things at once, thus splitting the doctor. This split perhaps has reference to the good and bad mothers of infancy. Statements are concrete. They refer to single isolated items, yet they are phrased to sound like valid generalizations. When pushed by anxiety, the patient resorts to archaic symbolic words and disruptive scrambled thoughts. He can and does put the therapist into situations in which anything the latter may say to the patient can be taken to mean one thing if it is the good doctor speaking and another if the bad doctor says it. "I hope you are feeling better" can mean either what it says or else that the therapist knows that the patient is not any better and is only uttering a pious, conventional phrase.

Another communicative technique which lends itself to schizophrenic testing and defensive uses is that of expressing feelings such as those of pain and rejection or fear or suspicion or anger, not in words, but by means of behavior which appears clinically as getting worse. Withdrawal and regression, impulsive outbursts, anything from catatonic stupor to catatonic excitement, may be the patient's only comment upon a broken appointment, a tactless remark, or the therapist's observed attention to another patient. There was a schizophrenic girl whose mother took her daily to see the therapist and called for her after the interview. Frequently when she called for the girl, the therapist and the mother would leave the girl standing by the car and walk away together for a few moments in order to talk about her. The patient never stated any resentment about this, but finally she expressed her rage and jealousy and hopelessness that her mother took even her therapist from her. The content of her feeling can only be speculated upon in retrospect, for the girl, as they walked away from her, cut her throat with a razor blade, so effectively that she died before they reached her. It is axiomatic that a therapist must never give his schizophrenic patient's time to a relative or put the patient in any desolate position which finds adequate expression only in murder.

The most difficult communication for me to learn to recognize, and the most useful when I do comprehend it, is that accomplished by a sort of sympathetic magic. The patient manages by means of words and acts to project into me his own feelings of futility, confusion, resentment, fatigue, and so on. It is as if he penetrates my conscious ego with his projections, which go into my preconsciousness and there set up a resonant response to the patient's feelings. This can be disconcerting, discouraging, and provocative of resentment. These are not good for the therapist or for the patient unless the therapist can recognize that they are a message and can use them to further his understanding and to clarify with his patient why the latter has to use this method rather than direct statements. If he does so, then there is revealed not only the patient's message but the further information that he is afraid of the therapist or is ashamed to anger him or feels guilty about hurting him or whatever else it may be that has prevented his communication. This clarification presents some testing of reality. The patient is brought to consider whether the therapist is actually dangerous, angry, injured, or, in fact, in no way damaged by the patient.

The thought presents itself that the schizophrenic complications of communication are a fact but that they are effective barriers to understanding only with the connivance of the therapist. It is also observed that the therapist need not understand everything his patient says; he needs only to pay attention, to be open to suggestion, and to keep in mind the need to clarify and structure the development of the therapeutic project. He must be alert to defenses and understanding of the patient's need for them. This understanding is first that the patient is gravely ill and in fear of dissolution. Therefore, he must keep his defenses available for a long time. He must be psychotic until he can afford not to be. The second understanding refers to the immediate defenses of the moment in treatment. It is desirable to find out what provokes a particular defense at a particular time. It is by dealing with the problem of the moment that the patient gets a little better put together and makes a little progress to a less generally anxious and defensive position.

The patient's ego resources, which need evaluation when his ability to profit from psychotherapy is considered, are so closely interrelated with one another that material presented from the life of a patient to document one of his resources serves equally well to reveal his other available resources. It is not one quality alone but the whole of his effective ego which indicates his availability in therapy. So it is possible to use these brief examples to indicate the extent of schizophrenic ability to observe the self and its doings. The splitting of the ego, which gives the condition its name, is apparent in that most of the patient's activity and speech shows his lack of awareness of his psychotic impediment. Yet there is also usually present, if only one can gain access to it, some part of the ego which perceives and is aghast at the pathological processes going on. Most of the crude symptoms of schizophrenia can be appreciated as the patient's attempts at restitution or, failing that, at least as an explanation of the loss of ego functions.

For the purpose of psychotherapy, based upon psychoanalysis, the self-awareness of the schizophrenic is in striking contrast to that of the psychoneurotic. That which the neurotic spends hundreds of hours of analysis discovering about himself, particularly his repressed infantile sexuality and his oedipal conflicts, his castration fears and her penis envy, the schizophrenic may tell his therapist in the first interview. In fact, if a patient does speak so readily of incest and matricide and such things, which to a normal person are unthinkable, one at once is alerted to the likelihood that he is a schizophrenic.

It is clearly not in this area of sexuality that the schizophrenic lacks awareness of his mental content. His repressed or split-off, "unconscious" content has rather to do with his peculiarities of thoughts and feelings. He does not know how to think about matters of immediate reality, how to grasp such a situation as that of being in a mental hospital and wanting to get out, how to think about a solution to this problem, or how to make a plan and carry it out. He does not recognize the functions of the hospital or the therapist in such a way as to make the best use of them to this end. Nor does he know that his feelings, so very appropriate to his sense of his situation, are quite inappropriate to the situation as others see it. Apart from some contributions from inherent ego tendency to split and regress, I do not know how to comprehend the unawareness of the schizophrenic except as a self-imposed restriction, of which he is unaware and which is meant to satisfy the interdictions of the presences of his parents. For purposes of therapy it follows that schizophrenic unawareness or avoidance of self-understanding is a variable which will be more troublesome when the therapist leads his patient into too threatening defiance of the presence. It will be least embarrassing when the therapist is able to respect the patient's devotion to the presence of the mother and to support him in steps toward reality in such a way that he does not feel forsaken and damned by her or by the therapist. I think that he will not get much better until he learns that doing so will not destroy his life-giving mother or his therapist.

This brings up the decisive importance of secondary gain from illness as a reason for failure in psychotherapy. From our nonschizophrenic or, to be more candid, our psychoneurotic or normal neurotic point of view, it may seem that the schizophrenic has given up his health for the prize gains of the joys of fantasy, the lazy and irresponsible status of a person who has to be taken care of by others, and the narcissistic omnipotence of thought and self-esteem which enjoys no corrective comparison with the facts of the real world. But this is probably little more than a projection of our own fantasy about our own escape from the responsibilities and disappointments in our real lives. It is not what schizophrenics, other than hebephrenics, seem actually to be getting out of their illness. The gain, if there be a gain, in schizophrenic living, seems to be that of the mother as a presence in the superego. The patient sacrifices himself to this presence. I, for one, do not believe that this is the ultimate in altruistic love. I believe that it is a desperate and bitter renunciation for the purpose of preserving the presence because the schizophrenic believes that the presence could, if it would, restore to the patient all that his infantile ego desires. I think that, when the schizophrenic patient enters and makes use of psychotherapy, he is motivated by a belief that the therapist can, by magic, help him force from the presence what is his due, namely, security to seek his own self-realization. The secondary gain from schizophrenia is the patient's illusion; it does not exist in fact. There is no real gain in the schizophrenic way of life.

What the patient legitimately desires can be, and usually is, forever lost through his persistent use of schizophrenic techniques meant magically to achieve it. Yet he cannot be expected to enter therapy with any techniques and aims other than these. Taken all together, they constitute his transference resistance. Before considering the therapist's responses to this apparent impasse, it is useful to try to pull together some of what we know of the schizophrenic's attitude toward life as we must expect it to appear in the transference resistance he brings to the therapist.

The underlying drive in the patient is to find in the therapist an all-satisfying and satisfied provider of all the supplies he needs and an understanding protector who, without tension, or anxiety, or anger, will happily remove from the patient all sources of discomfort, frustration, anxiety, or anger. The drive is to force the therapist to be a good breast, uncluttered by any disturbing attributes. Particularly, the therapist is to be an exclusive possession of the patient and is to find his own satisfaction exclusively in the existence of this one patient of his. The goal is a closed system of symbiotic bliss, utterly safe and gratifying.

Now this wish of the patient finds sympathetic response in anyone who feels positively for new-born babies. There is only one thing wrong with it. It is impossible of realization. You and I know that in the nature of things this goal is not to be achieved; only in modified terms of reality can it be approached. But the schizophrenic does not know about reality. He thinks his therapist could gratify him if he wanted to. Therefore, he tries to split the therapist into a good, co-operative one with whom the good patient can identify and a bad, destructive one on whom the patient can project all his own destructive impulses. In order to keep the illusion that the therapist is potentially supernaturally good, the patient tries to explain the therapist's failure to live up to expectations by assuming that it is because the patient is bad. If this badness could be eliminated, or concealed, then the therapist would love him adequately. The patient tries to eliminate or reduce or conceal all his feelings and impulses which might provoke the therapist. This endeavor obstructs communication and even threatens the relationship. Of what use is a therapist if you cannot desire anything of him or think anything about him or get mad at him? All the badness which the patient tries to dissociate from his attitude toward the therapist, if it is successfully split off from awareness, then tends to be available for projection onto the therapist.

No longer does the patient desire to suck or eat up the therapist. Rather, he feels that the therapist wants to suck or be sucked. No longer does he wish to destroy the therapist, but he senses that the latter is destroying him. Of course, these distortions justify in the patient a secondary, defensive layer of more or less justified resentments or righteous indignations. Either he withdraws, or in some more direct way he expresses his suspicions and feelings of persecution, of being exploited, influenced, and driven mad by the therapist.

There tends to be another layer of this attitude in which the patient feels guilty because of his ideas and impulses against the therapist. He is ashamed to report them and afraid of retaliation and rejection. He is also afraid that his ideas and impulses may magically destroy the therapist. Inevitable limitations upon the therapist's time and skill, which the patient experiences as disappointments, are interpreted by the patient as responses to his own hostility.

All these and the rest of the schizophrenic maneuvers in transference resistances are possible by reason of the patient's neglect of simple bits of reality, his refusal to value them. It is the function of the resistance to hold out against reality until the infantile fantasy is realized.

Before leaving this brief survey of schizophrenic transference-resistance phenomena, it should be noted that, if the therapist is competent, the relationship does persist, and bit by bit it introduces the patient to new experiences of such goodness as is possible in the real therapeutic situation. This is a poor substitute for a satisfactory actual childhood, but it is a vast improvement over what the patient has been used to finding in life. Consequently, his transference-resistance attitude and behavior will be modified by these moments of good relationship, and the patient will advance from his earliest infantile interest through the steps of childhood development. This advancement will be uneven and punctuated by regressions, each of which requires careful working-through to determine why it became necessary and what obstacle stands out as significant to the patient. When he arrives at the equivalent of normal adolescent behavior, there will be, as in normal adolescents, a revival of all the intensity of earlier phases of interest and conflict, and as a result of therapy the patient may well have become able to express a great deal of rebellion and aggression which was forbidden to him in his actual years of puberty. This can be a very difficult phase of treatment and one in which the patient's clinical picture seems to be shifting from that of a schizophrenic to that of a psychopath. It may be said, parenthetically, that a good many persons called "psychopaths" appear to be schizophrenics who have been stranded in this phase of partial recovery. This is therefore a stage in which it is particularly important not to desert the patient and to continue his treatment, however troublesome his behavior may be to himself and others.

Also, there will emerge in the transference, as treatment progresses toward conclusion, the outbreak of acutely intense conflicts about dependence-independence. This will mobilize the intense desire of the patient to be absolutely indispensable to the doctor and vice versa. Separation poses a terrific threat as well as an incentive to be free. This conflict will require much attention from the therapist. In a sense the patient is about to depart from his schizophrenic position, and he senses keenly the loss of the hope of ever finding the good mother–good baby symbiosis which has been his life's endeavor. He will certainly regard this situation as one imposed upon him by a rejecting and hostile therapist and will require particular working-through of his hostility to see upon what it is really based. What faces him as he leaves his schizophrenic, persecuted position is not healthy enjoyment of self-realization at all, at first, but principally some depression, some severe depression, helpless rage, and a feeling that reality is not worth the pain. The temptation to regress to the schizophrenic, persecuted situation, which offered, by way of further regression, a retreat to nirvana, is great. The therapist has a responsibility to stand by the patient through this phase of depression until he has learned to accept what is real and in actuality to prefer it to the illusions which have guided his life. Of course, his first acceptance of reality will be of relatively small fragments of it, and again there will be frequent regressions and retreats, but progress consists of working through each of these to further gain.

With this scanty outline of the general pattern of transference resistance in schizophrenia, it is proposed that the young psychotherapist shall learn the details by actually working, under supervision, with schizophrenic patients.

CHAPTER IX

Psychotherapy—the Therapist's Contribution

Earlier it was observed that, in the course of becoming a psychotherapist, one's attitude and understanding undergo considerable change. It is during the mastering of the general functions of a psychiatrist that this change gets under way, and it must proceed some distance before one is prepared to undertake intensive psychotherapy. As an example of the sort of modification which occurs in the thinking of a young psychiatrist, it can be noted that frequently he, the young psychiatrist, reacts toward hospitalized patients in very much the same fashion as do a good many of the laity. That is, if they are up and about, wearing their clothes, and being quiet, and if they converse at all rationally, he has the feeling that they are not psychotic. He becomes indignant that the authorities do not permit these patients to leave the hospital to pursue whatever at all reasonable-sounding aims they have in mind. Even quite acutely disturbed patients are excused to a considerable degree on the basis that they must be toxic or that something very disturbing has upset them. There is an obvious effort to deny the possibility of psychosis.

Sooner or later this attitude changes in the minds of

many residents into one in which it is assumed that practically everyone is more or less psychotic. It is evident that the relatives of patients are possessed of many of the same ideas and attitudes as the patients, and it is apparent that one's colleagues frequently fail to make sense. All together, the whole world appears to be on the verge of psychotic disorganization. This phase, fortunately, does not last either.

It is legitimate to wonder why these two exaggerated positions are so frequently assumed by those who first come in contact with psychotic patients. Among the probable reasons there stands high the fear of the fact of schizophrenia. The fact that one can be apparently fairly normal one day and the next day be in catatonic excitement is one which is resisted with great energy by anyone who has himself ever felt any insecurity about his sanity. This leads to the observation that a good many people have, at one time or another, been uncertain about their own stability. There is a most prevalent fear of psychosis. This fear accounts in part for the general aversion that people have for psychiatry and probably also for the fascination which it presents for some of us.

In the course of working one's way through the two phases in which it is believed that no one is psychotic or that everyone is psychotic, a resident does learn to recognize what is primary ego difficulty, what is secondary and in general restitutive in function, and what is not actually schizophrenic at all, although it occurs in a patient who suffers from the disorder. He learns also to recognize certain schizoid and schizophrenic processes in persons who are not, and probably never will be, psychotic. When recognition has been achieved that processes such as these go on in patients and in others, it follows also that some acknowledgment has been made to one's self that psychosis is a possibility, and one is a little less defensive and denying than he has previously been.

There is, however, a further defense. The young resident learns that the statistics are in favor of the patient. The majority of schizophrenic patients on the first admission tend to get materially better, and a very large proportion of them leave the hospital improved. This happens intrinsically or as a result of the atmosphere and the management of the hospital. The observation permits the resident a certain amount of peace of mind and gives him time to acquire some knowledge and judgment on which to base his satisfaction in his professional work. There is a further defense against accepting all the implications of the dynamics of mental illness. It is that the physical therapies are much in vogue and frequently clearly accelerate processes of restitution. Thus, as a detour, so to speak, the resident might devote quite a little time to mastering the techniques of physical therapy.

There is still a further defense against the full impact of the acceptance of schizophrenia as something which does exist and which can be terrifyingly destructive. This defense is an exaggerated interest in psychoanalysis and an effort upon the part of the resident to play the role of the detached, unfeeling, purely intellectual Freudian analyst, who listens to his patients and gets from what he hears material which can be translated into the theories of hysteria. I shall have something more to say about this matter later on.

At this point it seems advisable to insert a comment concerning the best way to set about becoming a therapist. One should select, for his training, a hospital in which it is possible to see at least a few patients over an extended period of time and for some time each week, so that some insight into the continuity of the patient's life may be achieved. It is important, also, that the hospital provide opportunity for supervision or for seminar discussions in a therapeutic atmosphere. These discussions and this supervision, if they are to be most valuable, will put as much emphasis upon the discussion of the behavior and the attitude of the physician as they do upon the pathology of the patient.

If this background can be achieved, then there is a further step which can be taken toward becoming a psychotherapist. I would urgently advise any resident beginning his training to subject himself to a rule. The rule is that he will not cure or analyze anyone during the first several months of his training. The purpose of this rule is to remove the temptation to do something rather than to be something in therapy. The temptation is strong to invade a patient's extremely precarious balance with the intention of doing him good but without the skill to avoid doing him harm. While one is under the rule not to cure anyone, it is quite in order that he should undertake to take care of patients—not only of patients but of their relatives and of hospital personnel. It is, of course, a good thing if he also takes care of his own mental hygiene at this time.

In the course of taking care of patients there are various situations to be met. There is the initial interview with the patient, held sometimes before his hospitalization, sometimes afterward. There are the admission procedures to which he is subjected, including learning from him his story of himself and his experiences, the taking of a mental status, the performing of a physical examination. There are the problems of adjustment to the hospital, there are the questions of transition from one service to another as the patient grows better or worse, and there are the steps and stages leading to discharge. In all these the physician has occasion to meet the patient in a two-person relationship. It is in this setting that he can undertake to acquire the essential attributes of a psychotherapist.

I would suggest that it is a good point to begin with that one pay attention to the psychology of two persons, one's self and the patient. What is going on in each person, what is each person trying to do, and what results from the effort of each—particularly, how does each respond to the other? Of course, it is not possible to assume a detached, observant attitude. One has to participate, to react, and only as an accompaniment to his activities observe what goes on. It will be necessary for most persons that a good bit of this self-observation be conducted after interviews with the patient rather than immediately during them.

Before undertaking even this step in training, it is necessary that a resident be advised to try to adopt a certain desired attitude and direction within himself. A primary requirement is that all his behavior should be in the interest of supporting the real ego of the patient. This means supporting such activities on the part of the patient as are realistic and valid and supporting the patient's self-esteem, his confidence in himself, and his ability to cope with his anxiety without resorting to regressive defenses. It is implied that supporting the patient's self-respect amounts to encouraging him to express himself and to give thought to his own self-interests and aims rather than exclusively to his symptoms or to the wishes and fears of other persons concerning him.

Upon undertaking some self-observation in the course of interviews with patients, one is almost certain to discover that, when the patient, according to his schizophrenic pattern, undertakes to split the therapist into at least two parts, there is a tendency on the part of the therapist to respond to this stimulus and to split himself into, on the one hand, a rational and realistic person and, on the other, a regressed, magical thinker. It is not likely that the regression will go so far as to suggest schizophrenia, but it is most likely that it will frequently extend to the level at which the physician finds himself acting in a childish fashion, indulging in wish-fulfilment and in efforts to dominate. He finds himself resenting helplessness, responding with anger and with guilt and with all sorts of defenses against these unpleasant states.

193

If one observes these things going on in himself, he is likely to try to escape by a resort to the defense of omnipotent fantasy or at least of the feeling of considerable power. Now, it is true that the physician has considerable ability to interfere with and retard and perhaps prevent the recovery of the patient. He has at least some modest power to facilitate the patient's recovery of his integration. However, in no sense is the physician a magical power. In no sense is he independent. He will discover time after time that his power operations aimed at the patient or personnel or relatives wind up, as does pride, in a fall. After a certain number of falls, one begins to doubt the usefulness of omnipotent fantasies about himself as a therapist. The truth is that the therapist is responsible to the hospital authorities and the public; he is at the mercy of relatives who may remove patients; and he is, after all, subject to his own limitations. It is not within his capacity to cure the patient, to bring about at will changes of any sort within his patient. What, then, does he do? There is no point in becoming depressed or feeling helpless. The answer, of course, is that he undertakes to increase his capacity for usefulness, usefulness to the patient in the little everyday things that make up the patient's comfort and security or fail to do so.

While the therapist is carrying on these very practical and simple duties, there is another great and growing area in which his usefulness can develop. In this area the psychiatrist tries to develop his ability to seek out and sort out facts. By "facts" one means those things which make a difference. If enough facts can be collected and can be sorted out, it becomes possible to grasp the situation in which the patient is and the direction of his movement, the pattern on which one can predict what will happen to him next. Some structure emerges in the physician's mind, which structure is to be kept in mind steadfastly. This is a good antidote to the tendency to get lost in the "schizophrenese" of the patient, to become fascinated by problems of communication and efforts to understand archaic expression. While this is a legitimate preoccupation in itself, it must be subservient to the general requirement that the physician continue to grasp what is actually going on in the patient and how this process may be structured beneficially. It becomes the physician's duty and privilege to clarify the situation, to strip it of a great many adventitious factors, and to present it in a comprehensible form.

The orientation of one who is trying to do this structuring will be that of attention to the ego of the patient, with the questions in mind: What does it understand of its situation, what does it want and fear, and how does it go about behaving in order to achieve its wants or annul its fears? What are its defensive, and what are its constructive, efforts, and in what way are these ambivalently bound together? If one can find some answers to these questions, then there is given some direction and sanity to the role of the therapist. He begins to grasp why he is in charge of the patient, how he can be helpful, and what he need not hope to do.

So far as the peculiar means of communication of the patient are concerned, this general orientation of the therapist tends to invite meaningful exchanges of information. It becomes more important to the patient to make himself understandable when he discovers that the physician has a genuine wish to understand something which might be of some use to the patient. Of course, one cannot treat a patient by means of conversation aimed endlessly at formulating the over-all general position and direction of the patient. This must be kept in one's own mind, but the conversation with the patient must be devoted to the present instance, to whatever is at the moment of concern to the patient. The point which needs to be kept in mind is that, however far the patient may digress, however much material may be presented which at the time seems unavailable for any use, one still keeps in mind the goal and that part of the path toward the goal which is at present important. One endeavors to maintain an optimum pressure upon this main issue. By "optimum pressure" one means that which will keep the patient working at it but which will not be so strong as to drive him away from it. Now, it would be foolishly optimistic to think that anyone can structure the problem of a schizophrenic and work steadily and consistently toward the solution of it. There will be, in spite of anyone's understanding and excellence of technique, situations in which the patient feels overpushed and reacts by regression. There will be other situations in which the physician fails to realize how much the patient is capable of doing, and allows a good bit of time to pass unprofitably.

Returning now to the assumption of the powerful role to which we have just referred, it needs to be noted that, if the physician is able to renounce this role and to be suitably modest in his expectations of himself, this will not of itself in any way stop the patient's expectations of magic. He will continue to expect the physician to be the all-powerful, good provider, the good breast, so long ago lost. When his expectations fail of achievement, he will tend, as indicated in the preceding chapter, first to take the blame onto himself and to continue to believe that the therapist is good. But eventually, when he is convinced that this method fails to get results, he will find it necessary to try to conceal his own badness. If he succeeds in dissociating it, it will then turn up projected onto the therapist.

It is not to be expected that the patient will advise the therapist at the moment that this occurs but rather that the patient will in some way show more evasiveness or defensiveness. It will be up to the therapist to be sufficiently in tune to sense what the patient is now thinking about him. In general, what the patient will impute to the therapist will be in the area of sexual material known to psychoanalysts as "perversity" or "infantile sexuality," or it will be in the area of destructiveness or malevolence.

One sufficiently sensitive to do psychotherapeutic work with schizophrenic patients is quite likely to sense, before he overtly hears about them, these attitudes which the patient has toward him. When he does sense that he is suspect, it is probable that he will react in ways which ordinarily we do not recognize in ourselves. In order to know what the patient is suspecting about him, a therapist needs to observe what goes on in himself. He needs to note when he begins to feel tense or anxious or guilty or ashamed, or when, if he is somewhat better acquainted with himself, he discovers that he is being a little exhibitionistic or voyeuristic or what have you.

When it becomes apparent that the patient is making some assertion concerning the perversity or the destructiveness of the therapist, the first question which comes up is not whether to admit or deny the accusation. Rather it is this: What is the patient trying to do by means of this accusation? The next question is: Why does the patient do this particular thing at this time?

Following this question, one may stop to ask how much truth there may be in the patient's accusation. The doctor undoubtedly knows how much truth there is overtly, but does he know, is he willing to find out, whether there is some unwitting behavior on his part justifying the patient's impressions of him? If, in the course of introspection, one discovers that there is a painful amount of truth in some belief the patient has concerning him—his integrity or his maturity or whatever it may be—then there is a further question. To what extent does this fact of immaturity in the therapist actually matter to the patient? Is it of a degree or in an area which makes it impossible to work with this patient? Or is it merely something which the patient has brought up and observed as part of his general self-protectiveness against potential enemies?

Of course, anyone who follows the course of training which is here being discussed will discover that he must abandon the idea that he is completely mature, well-integrated, and devoid of any unfortunate tendencies in his behavior toward others. However, this discovery does not mean that he is unsuited to be a therapist. It raises the question why the patient brings his accusation, and this we may perhaps discuss in two parts. First, when the patient makes an open accusation against the physician, what does he intend to accomplish? There are several possibilities. The imputation of certain infantile sexual interests may be an invitation coming from the patient's id, or it may be a test to see how reliable the doctor is or to find out how the doctor feels about infantile sexuality. It may be a clever maneuver to scare off the physician, to frighten him. As one considers these possibilities, one must wonder: Does the patient's technique achieve the desired effect? Does it, in fact, in any way tempt or seduce the doctor, distract him from his work, or in any degree frighten him away from any sort of intimacy, the necessary medium in which therapy occurs?

More commonly patients do not make open accusations against the physicians. They do it in an indirect fashion, frequently in an opposite fashion. For instance, the patient talks at some length about any form of perversity, let us say sadistic sexuality, to entertain his doctor. If the physician is gullible, he may think this is valid material coming from the patient, having to do entirely with the patient's background. Undoubtedly it is relevant to the patient, but it may be that there are more important things in the patient's mind which he can avoid by entertaining the doctor with accounts of his fantasies of cruel perversity.

There is another situation in which the patient makes his observations about the doctor in the third person only. He talks about someone else, sometimes someone somewhere else, occasionally someone in the present environment. The physician may be quite comfortable in listening to the patient who talks about the effeminacy of a colleague, unless he has discovered that the patient is not wasting any time talking about colleagues. What he is talking about is himself and the doctor who is present.

There are also ways in which the patient indicates what he thinks of the doctor by talking in quite opposite terms. It is possible that he talks at considerable length about the doctor's kindness, goodness, generosity, and self-sacrificing surrender to the requirements of his profession and shows a good bit of sympathy for the poor, hard-working physician. This may be one way of saying that the physician must be sadistic indeed in order to go to all this trouble to enjoy torturing his patients.

This whole area of the projection of the patient's tendencies onto his physician does seem to have validity for the patient, but it would appear also that very frequently these schizophrenic patients are keen diagnosticians of that which one does not see in himself. They often find a hook on which to hang their ideas, and, in general, since they need to defend themselves against closeness and intimacy with anyone, they devote themselves to serious efforts to keep the physician off balance and on guard. It becomes apparent that a physician who wishes to be most useful and successful in psychotherapy will have to become acquainted with himself, to know where and how large are the hooks on his personality on which patients may legitimately hang things.

It is my impression that practically all psychiatrists who would become competent therapists with schizophrenics need, for their comfort as well as for their efficiency, to be psychoanalyzed. This is not a point to be argued or debated or proved. It is merely a statement of opinion based on observation.

Yet there are a few exceptions. Certain persons are particularly talented in communicating with and getting along with and therapeutically influencing psychotic patients. Some of these physicians are most resistant to any sort of therapy directed toward themselves. One would suppose that they have a character defense in depth against a latent psychosis and that perhaps for their own comfort it is best to leave things as they are. The fact remains that they can be useful to patients, but this usefulness is practically always limited by their own scotomata, or blind spots. What one means specifically is that these physicians have limited goals and objectives for their patients. They tend to encourage the patient into the same sort of defensive and restricted position as that in which they keep them-

selves. I recall an example. There was a physician of unusual skill in making patients comfortable in a hospital;
he himself preferred to be a bachelor, living as close as
he could to the patients on the ward, and he saw no reason
why his patients should wish to leave. Many of them agreed
with him and became quite comfortably and permanently
settled in hospital life.

What is perhaps more important for the patient's good
than undue attention to his preoccupation with perversity
is adequate treatment of his problems of hostility, which,
for our purpose, we are considering in terms of his projection upon the physician. Hostility, as the patient senses
it in the physician, may be thought of in two ways. There
is first the perversion sadism, which often masquerades as
masochistic self-sacrifice; but there is a much larger area
in which schizophrenic patients are troubled by their own
hostilities and those which they sense in others, particularly
in their therapist. These are areas having to do with destructive impulses, anger, rage, resentment, contempt, indifference, and all the gradations of nonconstructive feeling.

The patient's unhappy belief that his therapist is motivated by nonconstructive impulses almost certainly rests
upon something concrete which he has observed in the
latter's behavior and which he has accepted as proof of
his suspicion. Two examples come to mind. One concerns
a patient who understood that he was to pay for and have
one hour of therapy five days a week. Perhaps the therapist did use the word "hour" when he made plans with the
patient. Actually he saw the patient for fifty minutes a

day. The patient became daily more silent, sullen, and suspicious. Then one day he looked at his watch as he came in, and again, pointedly, as he was about to leave the therapist. The latter noted this behavior and asked about it. Only then the patient reported that he had noticed he was cheated of ten minutes a day. He added that he at first thought it was carelessness on the therapist's part. Then he found that it occurred regularly and thought the therapist could stand no more of him. Then he watched the comings and goings of other patients who also were with the therapist only fifty minutes. He had concluded that the therapist was a thief, contemptuously exploiting his desperate victims. The clarifying of the situation not only prevented disruption of treatment; it brought into the open one of the patient's great difficulties, that of saying what he thought of anyone important to him. The other example is that of a man who spent three years in treatment with a therapist with whom he never talked about homosexual fantasies or his real marital difficulties. Referred to another psychiatrist, who asked about the meaning of the omission, the patient explained that he tried to tell these things but that his therapist always responded by restless moving in his chair, lighting a cigarette, and talking about something else. He added, "You know, Doctor, I think he was unhappily married and was afraid of homosexual seduction."

There is always the problem of recognizing that the patient is trying to convey a message at the same time that he tries to conceal it. If it can be brought into the open, it becomes necessary for one who would do psychotherapeutic work comfortably to become open-minded in considering the accusation that he is being destructive or in any way resentful, angry, and so on. The first reactions of most persons being accused of something of which they are not fully aware are denial and contrary assertion. This is, of course, a useless maneuver with a schizophrenic, merely serving to increase the distance between him and the therapist and thereby to decrease the possibility of therapeutic interaction.

It is certainly not necessary to discuss with a schizophrenic patient one's own personal difficulties. He has enough of his own and his relatives' to think of, but it is also important that one should not jump to self-defense and denial. It is possible, though, that in trying to avoid this denial, one fails to clarify the facts with the patient. This is a serious mistake. The patient has a right to know the fact. For instance, when he accuses the doctor of downright cruelty and vindictiveness, it is necessary for the doctor to acknowledge that certain things were done and that it is possible that he, the doctor, had some feeling of annoyance, but he does need to state flatly that he did not mean to torture the patient and to state positively that what he did, such as ordering wet-sheet packs, was for the patient's benefit. Rightly or wrongly, his intentions were therapeutic.

This brings up another distinction which it is important to learn to make: that between being nondefensive and being defenseless. As we use the term, to be "defensive" means to be denying something which is true, to be trying to evade and avoid it. This is something which one strives to eliminate in his work with patients. However, the opposite position is not that of being defenseless. It is not a problem of being defensive or defenseless. It is a problem of learning to dare to be realistic, to accept a fact, and to proceed from there. One's defense is one's own knowledge of his own integrity.

While discussing the various potential perversities and hostilities of the therapist, both actually present and imagined by the patient, it is important not to forget that, although the patient seldom says anything about it, the physician does have access to, and does present to the patient, certain virtuous attitudes. Among these are considerable modesty and humility and a seriousness and faithfulness which are perhaps a new experience to the patient. Also, the consistency of the doctor is an important therapeutic item. The fact that he keeps on regularly, month after month, becomes an impressive fact in the awareness of the patient. There are other such assets that one may manage to muster, if not constantly, at least during his therapeutic interviews. Something needs to be said about them.

The first observation is that schizophrenic patients have a way of saying very little about these things. They differ conspicuously from hysterical patients in their lack of immoderate admiration, affection, love, and so on, for their physician. One hears something about it by indirection, but, if one hears more than that about it, there is probably something being missed in the therapeutic situation. The patient has stumbled upon an adequate defense which the physician should eliminate by recognizing how he provokes it.

That the patient does not mention those qualities of his physician which he admires does not mean that he fails to note them. What he does with them is characteristically schizophrenic. He takes them in as if they were mother's milk, thereby incorporating some of the goodness which comes to be his own and upon which his ego feeds and grows. Thereby he measurably enhances his own self-esteem and self-confidence. One might suppose that for this he would be grateful, but again one hears very little about gratitude from these patients. What happens is that, in the process of taking in the goodness and incorporating it actually into himself, the patient manages to make the sort of split that is comfortable to all of us. He is good, and the badness is left with the doctor. Even the illness is left with the doctor. Sometimes it is quite striking that the patient comes to believe that the doctor is thoroughly psychotic, quite in the fashion in which he himself has been psychotic. The fact that this pattern frequently is repeated suggests that a physician should give some thought to maintaining his own self-esteem and integrity in the absence of any overt praise and appreciation and that he should be quite careful to search himself for masochistic satisfactions in being so narcissistically slandered by his patients.

It is important to modify what has been under consideration in the treatment of a schizophrenic patient by recognition that a great deal of what is important is related to quite superficial things. Schizophrenic patients do react, as we know, to tardiness or interrupted interviews or a state of illness in the physician, such as a common cold or a headache, or to the fact that the physician takes time off or that he pays some attention to someone else. Sometimes they react violently to these things. More particularly, they react unfavorably to weariness and indifference or to undue enthusiasm on the part of the doctor. It is important to keep these slight surface things in mind.

Also, it is necessary, as one comes to believe more firmly that the essential part of psychotherapy is carried on in the setting of transference, to remember that there is still something other than the transference of the patient to the doctor and also that the transference which the patient does have for the doctor has some relationship to what goes on among people who are in the environment. Thus, when the patient makes progress or slips, when he is in better or in poorer contact, when he communicates, in any way, distress or relief from distress, it is essential for the physician not casually to assume that this is all due to himself but to keep track of what is going on in the patient's life. This means to listen to nurses' observations and reports and to note what happens in the patient's relationships to relatives, to other patients, and to personnel. These matters can very well slip by and be ignored unless the physician remains alert to them. When they are investigated, it frequently comes as a surprise to the therapist that the fact that some other patient came into or left the hospital, a fact over which the therapist had no control, is interpreted by his patient as an intervention introduced by the therapist to influence the treatment. Sometimes the patient states that he thinks this is done for his good. One would suspect that he more commonly regards it as some sort of deception, not in his interest.

To summarize the point of view here being expressed, it might be said that it is extremely expensive in the course of psychotherapy with schizophrenic patients to permit any so-called "tacit" understandings to go unchallenged. These turn out most frequently to be misunderstandings, particularly on the part of the doctor. If they are brought into the open, they can be clarified; and, in the process of clarification, the doctor will learn something more of what a difficult person the patient finds him to be when it comes to communicating fully to him matters of serious importance.

The details on the surface are those with which one routinely works. They have reference to infantile meanings, and of course these are not choked off when the patient brings them up. The point is not to try to hammer away at the patient that what goes on currently is only a transference. So far as he is concerned, it is the bit of actual reality which he possesses. One keeps in mind constantly that, to the schizophrenic, the all-important matter is the tension which exists in a two-person relationship, the tension which prevents such intimacy as the patient actually craves and needs.

Earlier it was remarked that interest in the psychoanalytic approach as it applies to hysterical patients can well be a defense on the part of the physician which collaborates with that of the schizophrenic patient to avoid any mutual understanding of the basic problem of any sort of meaningful personal intimacy. Because it is so important and because I have observed so many mistakes made in this area, I wish to cite an example from the work of a colleague of the way in which sexual material comes out in the course of a spontaneous production of a schizophrenic patient who is in good rapport with his physician and of the way in which the physician deals with this content. It is in marked contrast to the way in which one would treat a psychoneurotic.

The account which I wish to give has unfortunately to be considerably disguised, and it is left to the reader's imagination to substitute some terms rather more expressive than those here used. It is hoped that the physician who made this report orally to me will record it in the literature in fuller detail.

This condensed report has to do with a young man who, somewhat late in his intensive treatment, which had been instituted because of an acute catatonic episode, awoke from sleep one night in panic about a dream. In this dream he encountered a jungle feline which lived in a "pit." He described this beast in all its horrible and terrible characteristics. According to his spontaneous account, this jungle feline was representative of a penis, and the pit represented a vagina. These two lines of associations were jumbled together, so that he said that the jungle feline was himself, it was his penis, it was his mother, and her penis, her vagina, it was full of all the penes in the world, and it sought to devour all of them. He further stated that it was filthy, fecal, putrid, stinking, bloody, *and fascinating*. In the fury of his revulsion (note the juxtaposition of *fascination* and *revulsion*) the patient asserted among other things that he hated his penis; he wanted to cut it off and be free forever from the jungle feline.

Being translated by the therapist, this impassioned outflow of words conveyed to him the idea that the patient felt that this penis of his, his sexuality, his very being and sanity, were all given to him in the process of birth. Thereby his mother had lost her penis. He saw himself as bound to his mother because his penis, his sexuality, his personality, and his sanity were all on loan from her. He visualized his mother's destructiveness if he were to permit anyone else to share in what he felt belonged to her. In the fury and terror of these associations, he actually perceived the doctor's office as literally filled with these jungle felines. The only solution he could devise to his state of panic was to cut off his penis. Unsaid, but inferred, was the thought that he could then return to his mother and be free both of her mortgage upon him and of her revenge. He could be again in peaceful symbiosis with her. It is worth noting that, although it also was not said, other productions of the patient on other occasions indicated that, having by this desperate self-mutilation freed himself from his mother, the patient would be able to enjoy real relationships, including the sexual, with other persons.

For all its concreteness, his expression "to cut off his penis" does not imply, in his magical thinking, that he will then be without one. However, in a situation such as this, there is a practical danger that the patient may mutilate himself.

What the therapist said to the patient at this time was stated quietly, firmly, and definitely. It was, "I do not believe you hate your penis. You like it. You need not cut it off." This brought this interview to a close. Of course, there was much later reference to this dream as treatment progressed toward the patient's freedom, confidence, and courage to live in the real world.

This dream is a striking sample of cryptic and symbolic schizophrenic thinking. It is fascinating to hear, and one finds it exciting to dare to imagine sufficiently freely to understand what one hears. At times the therapist's interest in symbols serves the patient as an interest in himself, but more likely he will be aware that the interest in the symbols is not in himself. He will probably be right if he assumes that undue interest in the symbolization is an evidence that the dream has stirred up in the therapist uncomfortable castration anxieties, which might induce him to defend himself by a flight into "psychoanalytic" theoretical interpretations to the patient. It should be emphasized that there is usually—one might say there is almost always—no place for an interpretation to the patient in the classical Freudian sense. What could we add to the jungle feline dream which would in any way make it more meaningful? There in its nakedness is a schizophrenic boy's deepest feeling about his mother's sexuality, his own sexuality, and the destructive relationship of his mother to him. The schizophrenia of it, as I see it, is to be found in the boy's readiness to emasculate himself in order to appease his mother's unconscious desires, envies, and punitive destructiveness toward males. This attitude of his mother, which he firmly believes does exist in her, of course was not stated to him by her in these terms. She had repeatedly been critical of his promiscuous father and bitter about sexuality in general and had vastly depreciated this boy child, whom she insisted on regarding as her darling and whom she brought up in a manner appropriate to a young lady.

The dream is about a beast and about genital organs. It is concrete—vividly, alarmingly concrete—but it must be understood also to refer to such things as his mother's character, her capacity to hate, his own dependency, his fear and need of her and of all her kind. The patient knows what it says about his insight into his mother. It would be tactless, crude, and impudent to tell him that. What he, near panic, does not know is that his actual penis is a prized part of himself, something to be protected. He must not cut it off. Nor may he escape his mother by cutting off his interest in persons, in women, in men (for he feared homosexuality also), or in his doctor. The concrete expression of opinion by the doctor that the patient did not hate his penis, that he loved it, covers all the ideas that we have just mentioned. They need not be elaborated at this time to the patient. He feels them, but he cannot verbalize them. This story is recounted to show that, although it is full of sexual symbols, its actual value, when produced by a schizophrenic patient, has to do with the deep-lying factors which prevent his comfortable intimacy with anyone and which cause him to regard himself as so undesirable because of his aggressiveness and masculinity as to lead him to thoughts of self-castration. It has something to do, of course, with his relation to the physician, which it is not appropriate to go into here, since, as stated, it is hoped that this physician will report the story himself.

It does bring us, however, to an observation that this patient was close to the end of his treatment. When one has been in a significant relationship with a schizophrenic patient over a considerable period of time, the problem of separation and termination is a real one, not only for the patient but also for the physician. The long habit of persistent effort in behalf of the patient has become somewhat fixed, so that it is actually something of a loss for the physician to have the patient depart. The therapist has invested much effort; he wonders whether the result is the best practically obtainable or whether he should try for more assurance against recurrence of illness. He questions whether the patient is really at the point of maximum benefit or whether he is leaving to escape some painful bit of unfinished work. So far as I know, there never has been a completed psychoanalysis of a schizophrenic patient! It is understandable that the decision to terminate therapy before arriving at theoretical completion is difficult yet necessary. To all this concern in the therapist's mind is added the knowledge that the patient tends to want to feel permanently indispensable to him, wants to realize a perpetually satisfying symbiosis. He will regard termination as a rejection. And he may react by quite violent recapitulation of his whole psychotic experience. This will have to be worked through. But there does come some point in treatment at which the therapist has to acknowledge that the patient may know best how much he can and will invest in the business of living in reality. There comes a point at which the therapist must accept the patient's goals, his morals, and, in general, his attitude toward himself and life. He must permit the patient to go and, I would believe, must always leave the door open for his return. It is my impression that, if his return is never blocked and if he is always welcome, that attitude on the part of the therapist will best serve the patient to continue to operate in the outside world and away from his physician.

Since it is implicit that one does not try to analyze all the positive transference—in fact, does not analyze any of it in these schizophrenic patients—one wonders what becomes of it when the patient has terminated treatment. As stated, some of it amounts to the patient's having eaten up some of the healthiness of the doctor so that he can build it into his own ego and thereby somewhat dispense with his dependence upon the superego and with his quest for the infant's long-sought breast.

There is a concrete example which comes to me of what one patient did with his therapist. Having been rather acutely ill for a matter of about two years, he eventually returned to the community, where he held a responsible job and lived with and supported his family. He got along to all appearances normally. Occasionally—that is, once or twice a year—this patient took upon himself to seek out the company of a man whom he knew to be a personal friend of his former therapist. In this setting he would inquire casually whether the man knew the therapist, and, upon being assured that he did, would say longingly that he wished he knew how to get in touch with that therapist. On each of the occasions, which occurred over a period of several years, the friend would reply that the therapist's telephone number was available and would offer to give it to him. The patient would thank him profusely and then would spend some twenty minutes talking and acting with all the mannerisms of his therapist so exaggerated that it became an impressive caricature of the latter. In the course of this procedure, he would treat the mutual friend quite as if the friend were himself a patient. With this twenty-minute re-enactment of the therapeutic relationship in reverse, the former patient would excuse himself and go his way. The friend reported these occurrences to the therapist, who expressed pleasure that the patient was doing so well and who reported to the friend that the patient never used the telephone number. He never communicated directly with him. There is no doubt, however, that the patient knew that the mutual friend reported these episodes. He kept the therapist at a discreet distance because he had deposited in the therapist all the worst of his psychosis. He kept him, through the casual mutual friend, potentially available because it was always possible that the psychosis might again invade him and that he might need the therapist. You might say that he might need the therapist to fight the devil with fire.